# CHELTENHAM in
# 100 OBJECTS

Cheltenham from Leckhampton Hill, *a lithograph by George Rowe, 1840. In the foreground is Tower Lodge, which still stands in Leckhampton Road. Cheltenham itself is dominated by Christ Church, which appears to tower above the terraces of Lansdown.*

This book is dedicated to Elisabeth Gemmill
in recognition of her thirty-five years as a volunteer
at Cheltenham Art Gallery & Museum, much of which
has been spent working on the local history collections
and object history files.

CHELTENHAM
ART GALLERY & MUSEUM

Produced with the assistance of
Cheltenham Art Gallery & Museum.

# CONTENTS

# ACKNOWLEDGEMENTS

FIRST AND FOREMOST, I wish to thank Jane Lillystone, Cheltenham Borough Council's Museum & Arts Manager, and the staff of Cheltenham Art Gallery & Museum for the opportunity to write this book. My particular thanks are due to Helen Brown, Kirsty Hartsiotis and Ann-Rachael Harwood for their constant encouragement, support and patience. I am especially grateful to each of them for arranging the photography of so many objects, and to Ann-Rachael in particular for her time spent scanning images. I am also grateful to Annik Brown and Bruce Barron for preparing objects for photography, and to Anna Stanway for copying images to disk.

The majority of the photographs in this book were taken by Michael Hall, and I wish to thank him for dealing so creatively with such a varied collection of objects. Unless otherwise stated, all images are from the Art Gallery & Museum's collections. Every effort has been made to trace the copyright holders of images used in the book and I would be happy to hear from anyone who believes that their copyright has been infringed.

CHELTONIA—" And there's still room."

*A cartoon by Ernest Webb, from the* Cheltenham Free Press & Cotswold News, *28 October 1899. Entitled 'The More the Merrier', it shows 'Cheltonia' placing the new Art Gallery on her mantelshelf, where it joins other important local buildings. (Reproduced by courtesy of Cheltenham Local & Family History Centre)*

A number of other institutions have provided both information and images, and I am particularly grateful for the help that I have received from the staff of Gloucestershire Archives and the Cheltenham Local & Family History Centre, and in particular Sue Constance, Paul Evans, Katrina Keir and Christopher Rainey. My thanks are also due to Jill Barlow and Christine Leighton at Cheltenham College; Kath Boothman at Cheltenham Ladies' College; Larry Hawks at the Pen Room (Birmingham); Karen Hull at the Jenner Museum; Tim Kershaw at the Jet Age Museum; Laura Kinnear and Sara Salvidge at the Holst Birthplace Museum; Shirley Park and Mirella Torr at Pate's Grammar School; Judith Ratcliffe at the Britten–Pears Library; David Reed at the Soldiers of Gloucestershire Museum; and Martin Watts at Cotswold Archaeology. All errors and omissions are, however, my own.

Many individuals have helped me, in so many ways, during the preparation of this book, and I particularly wish to thank the following: Alex and Sue Adlam, Ian Baker, John Baker, Sue Brasher, Terence Buckle, Michael Charity, Mrs J. Cheesman, David Elder, Beryl Elliott, Ann Ewart, John Fisher, Elisabeth Gemmill, Mike Hawkes, Jill Julier, John Keighley, Mick Kippin, Pam and Anna Linari-Linholm, Graham Lockwood, Neela Mann, Stuart Manton, Terry Moore-Scott, Hugh Nicholson, Geoff and Elaine North, Sylvie Pierce, Jacob Pot, Clive Relf, Nick Robertson, Peter Simmons, Jim Stevenson, Brian Torode, Christine and Tim Turton, Jill Waller, David Wilson, Gil Wakeley and John Whitaker.

Finally, I wish to thank Matilda Richards at The History Press for her guidance and support during the preparation of this book.

*Steven Blake, 2013*

Although some of the 100 objects featured in this book are on display at the Art Gallery & Museum, many others are held in the Museum's reserve collections, and are only shown occasionally, during special exhibitions. All of them are, however, available to view by prior appointment with the Museum's Collections Manager, who may be contacted on 01242 387492 or by email at collections@cheltenhamtrust.org.uk. To find out more about the Museum, its collections and its activities, please visit www.cheltenhammuseum.org.uk

# INTRODUCTION

CHELTENHAM HAS HAD museums and museum collections for more than 200 years, the earliest known being a 'Cheltenham Museum of Natural and Artificial Curiosities' in the High Street that the Finnish artist, Jacob Spornberg, advertised in the *Cheltenham Chronicle* during 1810, although neither its content, nor how long it lasted, is known.

Six years later, in 1816, the mineralogist John Mawe and his son-in-law, Anthony Tatlow, opened a museum to the south of the Montpellier Spa, at which rocks, minerals and shells were displayed (and sold) to visitors, along with items made from them, such as statues, vases and inlaid tables.

That lasted until 1843, when it was closed and demolished to make way for the Montpellier Exchange, now a branch of Barclays Bank.

Three years earlier, in 1840, one of England's most important collections of old master paintings, the property of Lord Northwick, had opened to the public at his Cheltenham residence, Thirlestaine House. It remained a major attraction for visitors to the town until 1859, when it was closed, and the collection sold, following Lord Northwick's death.

The Cheltenham Literary & Philosophical Institution (founded in 1833) maintained a museum 'of natural history, antiquities and works of art and science' at its premises in Promenade Villas between 1836 and the Institution's closure in 1860. Thereafter, the collections were transferred to Cheltenham College, which opened a museum in 1871, with the Cheltenham Ladies' College following suit in 1887.

Both College museums focused on natural history and geology, as well as displaying some of the many gifts that were presented to the

*The earliest dated view of the town:* The West Prospect of the Spaw and Town of Cheltenham, *by Thomas Robins, 1748. Against a somewhat exaggerated Cotswold backdrop may be seen the houses of the old market town, with the medieval St Mary's Church to the left and the spa well and Well Walk to the right.*

*A detail of a panoramic view of Cheltenham from the roof of Cheltenham House, the former Cheltenham & Gloucester Building Society offices in Clarence Street, by Richard Parker Crook, 1984. Among the most prominent buildings are the tower of the Public Library and the churches of St Matthew and St Gregory. (Reproduced by courtesy of the artist)*

Colleges by former pupils and others. Cheltenham College Museum was regularly open to the public, but the Ladies' College Museum was not, being purely an educational resource for the College itself. Both museums were eventually closed, and much of their collections were dispersed.

A number of privately-owned subscription libraries were established in Cheltenham from 1780 onwards, and in 1884 a Free Library, funded by the Borough Council, was opened in temporary premises in the High Street. That was replaced in 1889 by a purpose-built Library and Schools of Art & Science in Clarence Street, on the east side of which an Art Gallery was added in 1899, following Baron de Ferrieres's bequest to the town of forty-three Dutch and other northern European paintings, along with £1,000 towards the cost of a gallery in which to house them.

Cheltenham Library still occupies the ground floor of the 1889 building, but the Schools of Art & Science, which occupied the upper floor, moved out in 1905 and were replaced in 1907 by the Museum, which still occupies those rooms, along with an extension that was opened on the site of the 1899 Art Gallery in 1989.

Between 1929 and 1945, three adjoining premises, immediately to the east of the Art Gallery, were acquired for museum and library use. Two of them (53-55 Clarence Street), along with three small cottages to their rear in Chester Walk, were demolished in 2011 to make way for a further extension, to which 51 Clarence Street, part of an early nineteenth-century terrace known as Bedford Buildings, will be connected.

Even before the opening of its Museum, the Borough Council had begun to collect museum objects, which were presumably stored (and perhaps even displayed) in the Public Library. The earliest of these relating to the town's past were the 'weighing chair' from Williams's Library and the Dowdeswell Pike, which were acquired in 1896 and 1899 respectively. By 1907, the embryonic collection also included a number of local paintings, prints, medals and tokens.

Since 1907, the Art Gallery & Museum (which is simply referred to hereafter as 'the Museum') has continued – and still continues – to collect material relating to the town's past. Its local collections are now particularly rich in paintings, drawings, prints and photographs; books and printed ephemera; local archaeology; numismatics; ceramic and wooden souvenirs; metalwork; costume (particularly from local shops); 'personalia' connected to notable residents and visitors; architectural models and items relating to sport, industry and transport.

Much of the collection has been generously donated by private individuals, many of them Cheltenham residents, while a smaller number of items have been purchased, either privately or at auction. Their acquisition has been funded from the Museum's purchase fund, provided by the Borough Council as part of the Museum's annual budget, and from a number of generous financial bequests that have been made to the Museum over the years.

Wherever possible, additional funding has been obtained from such organisations as the NACF's Art Fund, the Government Purchase Grant Funds administered by the Victoria & Albert and Science Museums, the Friends of Cheltenham Art Gallery & Museum and a number of Charitable Trusts.

This book seeks to demonstrate the richness and variety of the Museum's local collections by highlighting 100 objects that reflect the history of the District (including Charlton Kings, Leckhampton, Prestbury and Swindon Village, as well as Cheltenham itself) from prehistory to the twentieth century.

Choosing just 100 objects has been no easy task, and an attempt has been made to balance the need to cover as many aspects of the town's past as possible with a desire to include the collection's more 'iconic' or visually interesting items. A decision has also been made to limit the choice to three-dimensional items and printed ephemera, and to exclude paintings, prints and photographs of the town on the grounds that these have so often been reproduced in other local history books – although examples of all of these (including a number from other public and private collections) have been included as 'supporting images' where they help to illuminate an object's story.

*The first page of the Art Gallery & Museum's earliest Accessions Register, recording the donation of the weighing chair from Williams's Library in 1896 and of the Baron de Ferrieres collection of northern European paintings in 1899.*

The text accompanying each object seeks to explain its context and/ or significance in the history of the town and to provide some detailed information about the object itself. In researching each object, the relevant entry in the Museum's Accessions Registers, in which every item entering the collection is recorded, and in each object's own history file, in which relevant information is stored, have proved invaluable.

Another important source of information has been the many books and articles on the history of Cheltenham that have been produced since the mid-nineteenth century, including the publications of the District's local history societies, which contain a wealth of previously unpublished information.

Equally important are a range of primary printed sources that are held at Cheltenham Library's Local & Family History Centre, most notably newspapers, directories and guidebooks, and the extensive manuscript collections relating to Cheltenham at Gloucestershire Archives. A number of websites, such as 'Ancestry', enable easy access to census returns and to records of births, marriages and deaths.

Perhaps the ultimate aim of this book is to demonstrate the value of museum objects in understanding our past. Only the reader will be able to judge whether that aim has been achieved – and the observant reader will certainly note that there are many aspects of the town's past that have not been covered, either through lack of space or lack of relevant objects. For as well as adding valuable new information to the Museum's object history files, preparing this book has highlighted the gaps in the local history collections, particularly as far as objects relating to present-day Cheltenham is concerned, and will hopefully help the Museum to develop its local history collecting policy for some time to come.

*Steven Blake, 2013*

# one **EARLY CHELTENHAM**

EVIDENCE FOR HUMAN activity within the present Cheltenham District dates back to the New Stone Age (3500-2000 BC). It is represented by a number of chance finds of stone implements, flints and pottery, mainly from Arle, Charlton Kings, Leckhampton and Prestbury – and by some evidence that a prehistoric burial chamber once stood in the vicinity of St James's Square, until it was destroyed when the Great Western Railway was being constructed in 1846.

*Painted Romano-British wall-plaster and a fragment of an apothecary's palette from Vineyards Farm, Charlton Kings.*

Since the 1970s, excavations across the District have provided significant new evidence for occupation during the Bronze Age (2000-700 BC), Iron Age (700 BC – AD 43) and Romano-British (AD 43-410) periods. This includes Iron Age boundary ditches at Arle Court and at the site of the Junior Library in Chester Walk, and Iron Age pits and pottery at Vineyards Farm, on the slopes of Wistley Hill above Charlton Kings, and at Brizen Field, Leckhampton. Excavations at the last two sites also revealed evidence of Romano-British settlement; at Vineyards Farm the remains of a substantial three-roomed building with surviving fireplaces, and fragments of painted wall-plaster and roof tiles were uncovered during excavation in 1980-1984. These sites also yielded a range of small finds, such as bracelets, brooches, coins, pottery and, at Vineyards Farm, a fragment of an apothecary's palette made from Pyrenean marble, which would have been used for grinding medicines.

Since 1997 further evidence of Romano-British settlement has been found closer to the town centre, at West Drive, Pittville, and on the site of the new Waitrose store, close to St James's Square, where excavations revealed two human burials, some pottery and elements of a field system sloping down to the River Chelt, perhaps associated with a settlement (possibly a villa?) on the light, well-drained Cheltenham Sands, close to the Lower High Street.

ALTHOUGH THERE IS no firm evidence of any continuity of occupation between the Romano-British and Anglo-Saxon (AD 410-1066) periods, excavations at the former Kingsmead School (now All Saints' Academy) site in Hesters Way during 2009-2010 revealed evidence of occupation from the sixth to the eighth century, including pottery and traces of a large timber hall. Although the finds are (at the time of writing) with the excavators, Cotswold Archaeology, they will eventually be donated to the Museum, including this, probably sixth- or seventh-century vessel, which has a slight footstand and one remaining pierced lug.

*An Anglo-Saxon pot from the Kingsmead School/All Saints' Academy site, Hesters Way. (© Cotswold Archaeology)*

During this period, Cheltenham was part of the kingdom of Mercia, and was ruled by a tribe known as the Hwicce. The earliest documentary evidence for a settlement on the site of the town occurs in AD 803, when a dispute between the bishops of Hereford and Worcester over who was entitled to the revenues of a minster church ('monasterium') at Cheltenham was settled at the Council of Cloveshoe: whether or not that church stood on the site of the present St Mary's Church is uncertain.

Late Saxon Cheltenham was a Royal manor, which it remained for some time after the Norman Conquest. In 1086, when the Domesday Book was compiled, the manor of 'Chineneha' comprised eight and a half hides of land (anywhere between 1,000 and 2,000 acres) and had five mills along the River Chelt. The adult male population of the Cheltenham Hundred (more or less equivalent to the modern District) in 1086 has been estimated at 114.

IN ADDITION TO Cheltenham itself, the present District includes a number of other early settlements, four of which – Charlton Kings, Leckhampton, Prestbury and Swindon Village – were independent parishes by the twelfth century.

*A group of medieval roof tiles from the site of Prestbury Manor House.*

Few houses within the District – apart from The Priory at Prestbury and Leckhampton Court – retain significant medieval fabric, but excavations have revealed the sites of moated manor houses at Leckhampton and Prestbury. The manor house at Prestbury, about a quarter of a mile north-west of the church, was owned by the bishops of Hereford from at least the twelfth to the sixteenth century, when it passed into secular ownership. Finds during the excavation of its site in 1937-1939, and again in 1951, included stonework, coins, pottery, glass, floor tiles and roof tiles, such as this group of probably fourteenth-century glazed earthenware ridge tiles.

Although now partly built over, the outline of the Prestbury Manor site may still be seen on the north side of Park Lane, overlooking Cheltenham Racecourse, which occupies the site of the bishop's deer park.

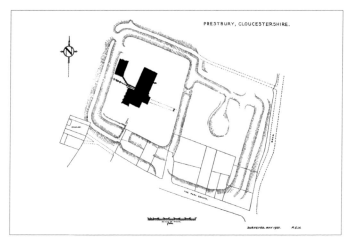

PRESTBURY, GLOUCESTERSHIRE.

*A plan of the Prestbury Manor site by F.C. Vickery, published in the* Transactions of the Bristol & Gloucestershire Archaeological Society *in 1956, showing its two rectangular moats, surrounded by a continuous earthen bank.*

*A limestone carving of the rose window in St Mary's Church.*

EACH OF THE District's five medieval churches retains something of its medieval fabric, although all were subject to drastic restoration or rebuilding during the nineteenth century. Cheltenham's St Mary's Church, with its adjoining churchyard cross, is the town centre's only surviving medieval building and is distinguished by its fourteenth-century 'Decorated' style window tracery, and in particular by one of England's finest examples of a circular 'rose window'.

This beautifully carved limestone model of the rose window, which has a diameter of five inches, was given to the Museum in 1960. Although neither its date nor its carver is known, one possible clue to its date is the fact that the wooden stand in which it is mounted has, pasted on its reverse, a print of St Mary's Church cut from J. Joyner's *Cheltenham Past and Present*, which was published in about 1900; a copy of this print is shown above.

*Two examples of a trade token issued by Thomas Mason, 1669.*

THE VILLAGE OF Cheltenham became a market town in 1226, and the market – along with agriculture – remained the basis of its economy until the early eighteenth century. It also had a range of urban occupations, and some industries, including the manufacture of cotton stockings, and, for a time in the seventeenth century, the growing of tobacco. In 1249, Prestbury also became a market town, but was too close to Cheltenham to prosper, and its market appears to have ceased after a major fire in The Burgage in about 1500.

The Museum has a small number of items from seventeenth-century Cheltenham – these include a copper bed warmer inscribed with the name of Thomas Cox and the date 1685, and examples of the copper tokens that were issued by at least nine Cheltenham and one Charlton Kings tradesmen between 1652 and 1669, as a form of local currency during times when coinage was in short supply. The example shown above is a halfpenny dated 1669, and bears the initials 'T M M'. Its diameter is 20mm. The most likely candidate for its issuer is a hosier named Thomas Mason (died 1711), the second 'M' no doubt referring to his wife Mary.

The Masons were a prominent local family, another of whom, a mercer named John Mason, also issued a halfpenny token, in 1667. Thomas the hosier was probably the father of the William Mason who owned the field in which the spa waters were first discovered; William's daughter Elizabeth later married Captain Henry Skillicorne, who is regarded as the 'founding father' of the Cheltenham spa.

*A badge and two buttons from a Cheltenham Charity School uniform.*

*(Reproduced by courtesy of Gloucestershire Archives P78/1 Sc 1/9/1)*

DURING THE SIXTEENTH and seventeenth century, Cheltenham acquired a number of public buildings and institutions, including a market house, a jail, an almshouse and a grammar school. A second school, for poor boys, was established by one George Townsend in 1683, and was re-founded in 1713 by a group of subscribers led by Lady Capel. Known as the Charity School, it met in a room above the north porch of St Mary's Church between 1729 and 1847, when a new school was built for it in Devonshire Street; by then it was known as the Parish Church Boys' School.

The school was also sometimes known as the Blue Coat School, after the pupils' blue uniforms, which had brass buttons bearing the date 1713. Each pupil also wore a brass badge with the date 1713; examples of both of these are shown above, and they may be seen being worn in the adjoining photograph of some of the pupils and their teachers, taken in 1865.

*A painted fan by Thomas Robins,*
*showing the spa well.*

CHELTENHAM'S SPA WATERS were first discovered in a field to the south of the town (the site of which is now occupied by Cheltenham Ladies' College) in 1716. The field's owner, William Mason, fenced the spring and began to charge for the waters, but it was not until 1738 (fifteen years after Mason's death) that the embryonic spa was put on a commercial footing, after his son-in-law, a retired sea captain named Henry Skillicorne, had moved to Cheltenham with his wife, Elizabeth.

Between 1738 and 1742, Skillicorne deepened the spring to form a well, installed a pump and built a brick shelter above it, from which the 'subscribers' could be served the waters. He also built a small assembly room to one side of the well, and planted tree-lined avenues to the north and south of the well, known as the Well Walk, which connected the well to the town via a small bridge across the River Chelt.

This view of Skillicorne's new spa well was probably painted in 1740 (before the planting of the 'lower walk', north of the well) by Thomas Robins (1716-1770), a fan painter from Charlton Kings who later went on to become a successful painter of landscapes and 'gentlemen's seats'. Also shown are the Great House, the home of Lady Stapleton, and St Mary's Church. Seated on a bench at one end of the Walk is a small figure sketching, which is presumably meant to represent Robins himself; this detail is shown above right.

This is one of two fans by Thomas Robins in the Museum collection, both showing the spa well. It was purchased at auction in 2012, with financial assistance from the Art Fund.

*An engraved dial from a clock by Moses Bradshaw of Charlton Kings.*

SEVERAL CLOCK AND watch makers worked in the District during the late eighteenth and nineteenth century, including Moses Bradshaw of Charlton Kings, for whom this brass dial from a thirty-hour long-case clock was engraved, probably in Bristol, during the 1770s.

Moses Bradshaw was almost certainly the son of a Northleach farmer of the same name who had settled at Leckhampton, where Moses junior was baptised in 1751. By the 1760s Moses senior had moved with his family to Charlton Kings, where his son is recorded in the churchwardens' accounts as having been paid to clean and repair the church clock on various occasions between 1774 and 1795. Moses junior died at Charlton Kings, aged eighty-nine, in 1841.

This is one of two known dials to bear Moses Bradshaw's name, the other – which also shows a river scene – being in a private collection. The Museum also has, on loan from the Michael Grange Collection of clocks at the British Museum, a complete eighteenth-century longcase clock by Richard Petty of Cheltenham, with a similar engraved dial, showing some cottages and a church with a spire.

*A miniature portrait of John Boles Watson, Manager of the Cheltenham Theatre.*

CHELTENHAM'S EARLIEST THEATRE had been established by 1758 in a converted malt house in Coffee House Yard, the site of which is now occupied by part of Pittville Street. In 1779, it was acquired by an Irish actor turned theatre manager named John Boles Watson (1748-1813), who opened a new, purpose-built theatre in York Passage (now Grosvenor Terrace) three years later. It was there that King George III attended several performances during his 1788 stay in the town, causing it to be renamed the Theatre Royal. In 1805 this was replaced by a larger theatre in Bath Street, Cambray, which remained in use until it was burnt down on 3 May 1839.

Watson was one of the most successful theatre entrepreneurs of his day; at its height, his theatrical 'circuit' comprised no less than forty-four theatres across Wales and the Midlands.

This oval miniature portrait of Watson, the reverse of which bears the date 1812, is contained within its original ivory case. Although unsigned, it has been suggested that it might be the work of an Irish miniaturist turned actor named Alexander Pope (1763-1835), who is known to have performed at Watson's Cirencester theatre in 1811.

*Three Bilston enamel 'toys', produced as souvenirs of Cheltenham.*

AS THE NUMBER of visitors to Henry Skillicorne's spa well increased, so too did the demand for souvenirs of Cheltenham. From as early as the 1740s, the spa waters were bottled for sale, and they could be bought as far away as London and Bristol. In 1781, the first guidebook to Cheltenham was published, followed in 1786 by the first engravings of the town, showing the Well and Well Walk. Soon after, similar engravings were being used for circular or oval 'watch papers', which were placed inside watch cases as a souvenir of the town.

The earliest three-dimensional souvenirs of Cheltenham appear to be a number of small late eighteenth-century enamelled boxes produced at Bilston in Staffordshire, an important centre for enamelled wares from the 1740s. These were often known as 'toys' and bore the name, or a view, of the town in which they were to be sold. They were generally used to contain snuff or (if they had a mirror inside), the small black fabric 'patches' that were used to cover up skin blemishes.

These three Cheltenham examples – one of which shows the Well Walk – would have been sold in the shops of the High Street, or in the temporary booths that tradesmen from London and Bath are believed to have established close to the spa well during Cheltenham's fashionable summer season.

*Queen Charlotte's copy of the 1788 edition of Moreau's* A Tour to Cheltenham Spa.

IN 1780, SIMEON MOREAU, from Bath, became Cheltenham's first 'Master of the Ceremonies', in which role he presided over the social life of the Assembly Room in the High Street. In 1783, he published Cheltenham's second earliest guidebook, *A Tour to Cheltenham Spa*, revised editions of which appeared in 1786 and 1788.

In the summer of 1788, King George III, Queen Charlotte and three of their daughters spent five weeks at Cheltenham so that the King could drink the spa waters in an attempt to cure the effects of 'a pretty smart bilious attack' that he had suffered earlier in the year. On their arrival in Cheltenham, Moreau presented the Royal party with copies of his guide; it is clear, however, that Queen Charlotte already had a copy, presented to her as a gift by Lady Courtown, whose husband was Treasurer of the Royal Household. Lady Courtown had certainly been in Cheltenham in late June 1788, when the Queen wrote to her asking her to secure three pews in St Mary's Church for the duration of their intended visit.

What happened to the Queen's copy of the guide after 1788 is unknown, but in 2004 it was purchased at auction by the Museum. Queen Charlotte's bookplate is pasted on the inside of the cover, and on the opposite page is written, in the Queen's own hand, 'Lady Courtowns gift on the Day of our arrival, the 12th/July 1788', followed by the words 'The Queen'.

A

# TOUR TO CHELTENHAM SPA;

O R,

## GLOUCESTERSHIRE DISPLAY'D.

CONTAINING

### AN ACCOUNT OF CHELTENHAM,

IN ITS IMPROVED STATE;

ITS

| MINERAL WATER, | AMUSEMENTS, |
| PUBLIC WALKS, | ENVIRONS, &c. |

THE

### NATURAL HISTORY OF THE COUNTY AND CITY OF GLOUCESTER,

AND THE TOWNS OF

| CIRENCESTER, | TEWKESBURY, |
| TETBURY, | FAIRFORD, &c. |

### A CORRECT ITINERARY FROM CHELTENHAM.

AND AN

Account of the Posts from *Gloucester* and *Cheltenham*, agreeable to the latest Regulations.

The Whole interspersed with Explanatory
HISTORICAL, CHRONOLOGICAL, and GENEALOGICAL NOTES,
Carefully selected from the best Authors.

THE THIRD EDITION.

B Y

SIMEON MOREAU, M. C. CHELTENHAM.

B A T H:
Printed for the AUTHOR, by R. CRUTTWELL;
And sold by Him, and all the Booksellers in Bath; Mr. HARWARD, at Cheltenham, Gloucester, and Tewkesbury;
And by C. DILLY, Poultry, and J WALTER, Charing-Cross, London.
M DCC XXXVIII.

*The title page of Moreau's 1788* A Tour to Cheltenham Spa.

DURING THEIR STAY in the town, the Royal party went regularly to the spa well to take the waters, and attended the Assembly Room, the Theatre and St Mary's Church. Although the King appeared to flourish during his stay, which ended with the Royal party's

*Two examples of the 1789 Royal Cheltenham and Restoration Medal.*

return to Windsor on 16 August, his illness – now believed to have been porphyria, a liver disease that induced symptoms of madness – recurred during the winter of 1788/89, and his recovery in February 1789 was a cause for national rejoicing.

Simeon Moreau had planned to commemorate the Royal visit by issuing a medal, but unfortunately two successive dies for the medal were broken, by which time King George had fallen ill and the project was 'put on hold'. Following the King's recovery, a decision was made to commemorate this as well as his visit, and this medal, which was struck by Messrs Hancock & Phipson of Birmingham on 23 April 1789, was the result. Gold and silver versions were produced, and examples were presented to members of the Royal family, the British Museum and the Universities of Oxford and Cambridge.

One side of the medal, which has a diameter of 43mm, shows the spa well, with the date 1788 and the words *Ob Salutem Restauratam* ('on his restored health'). The other side shows Hygeia, the goddess of health, with a serpent and a young oak tree (both representing longevity) and a medallion showing a cameo portrait of the King. It bears the date 1789 and the words *Georgio III Optimo Principi* ('to the most excellent Prince George III').

*The Royal party in the Assembly Room, an engraving published in 1788. Perhaps the figure bowing to the King is meant to represent Simeon Moreau?*

*A ceramic flowerpot with a profile of King George III.*

KING GEORGE III had originally planned to return to Cheltenham in 1789, but following his winter illness he was advised to try sea bathing at Weymouth instead, and he visited that town regularly until 1805.

Although the King never returned to Cheltenham, his visit did much to enhance the reputation of its spa waters, and both the number of visitors and the town's population continued to rise: in the 1801 census its recorded population (excluding the outlying villages) stood at 3,076 and the number of its houses at 710, both around double the estimated figures of eighty years before. King George's visit was certainly not forgotten, and when this souvenir flowerpot was produced by the Coalport factory in Shropshire, possibly for the 1809 Jubilee, it carried a profile portrait of the King and the inscription 'A token from Cheltenham'. Unfortunately, its separate base has not survived.

Large numbers of souvenir ceramics, mainly with transfer-printed views of the town, were produced for sale to visitors to Cheltenham from the late eighteenth century onwards. They were commissioned from factories as far away as the Staffordshire Potteries, presumably by Cheltenham tradesmen, and often used existing topographical prints as a source of illustration. The Museum has a very fine collection of such souvenir ceramics.

# three **THE NINETEENTH CENTURY**

BETWEEN 1793 AND 1815, Britain was at war with Revolutionary and Napoleonic France. Cheltenham has an unusual reminder of that conflict in the so-called Imperial or Napoleon Fountain, which was installed next to the newly-built Imperial Apartments on the south side of Imperial Square in 1997, following its restoration by Nimbus Conservation, funded by Beaufort Homes.

The fountain is made of marble and shows a cherub grasping a swan's neck, balanced on an orb with three more cherubs' heads, below which are three bowls in the form of shells, atop three dolphins, with a wider bowl below, and a rocky base, from which small reptiles emerge.

The fountain is first recorded in Cheltenham in 1826, when it was placed in a small pavilion to the east of the Sherborne or Imperial Spa, which stood on the site of the Queen's Hotel between 1818 and 1837. According to contemporary newspaper reports, the fountain was the work of an eighteenth-century Italian sculptor named Cesario Bruni (of whom no record appears to exist!) and was looted from Genoa by Napoleon's army in about 1800, subsequently captured at sea by an English privateer, and eventually purchased by a Cheltenham lawyer, Thomas Henney, who was the co-owner of the Sherborne Spa.

Since 1826 the fountain has had a remarkably chequered history. In 1834 it was transferred to the Montpellier Gardens, where it remained – and gradually deteriorated – until 1902, when the Borough Council, which had acquired it when it purchased the gardens in 1893, sent it to R.L. Boulton & Sons for restoration. Thereafter it was sited in the Town Hall (1906-1925) and the Public Library (1926-1964), before being put into storage.

Eventually, in 1986, it was 'rescued' from oblivion and re-assembled for a time at the Montpellier branch of Lloyds Bank, before being removed to storage once more, until the opportunity to install it in its current location arose.

*The Imperial or Napoleon Fountain after its restoration by Boultons in 1902-1903.*

*The fountain in its pavilion close to the Sherborne Spa, near to where it now stands, a lithograph by R. Mckay, 1827.*

*The fountain in Montpellier Gardens, a steel engraving by George Phillips Johnson, 1836.*

*General Lefebvre-Desnouettes's gold ring.*

Right *General Lefebvre-Desnouettes, a stipple etching by Charles Aimé Forestier, about 1807, probably after a portrait of the General by H. Weingandt. (© The Trustees of the British Museum)*

DURING THE NAPOLEONIC WARS, a number of French prisoners-of-war were paroled to Cheltenham. Among them was General Charles Lefebvre-Desnouettes (1773-1822), who had been captured in Spain in 1808. He, two other French officers and several soldiers arrived in Cheltenham in February 1811 for what was clearly a comfortable stay, during which the General and his wife (who joined him in Cheltenham) were welcomed into the town's fashionable circles.

One of those who befriended the General was Francis Welles of Marle Hill, who is said to have loaned him money with which to clear some debts – as a surety for which the General left with him a watch and this superb gold ring, which is decorated with grape vines and has a 'hidden' compartment with a cameo portrait of Napoleon. The money was, however, used by the General to finance his escape back to France in May 1812, after which he rejoined the Emperor's army and fought in a number of campaigns, including Waterloo in 1815. After the fall of Napoleon he fled to America, where he helped found a colony in Alabama; he lived there until 1821, when he decided to settle in Holland, but he drowned in May 1822, when the ship in which he was travelling sank off the Irish coast.

The General's watch has never come to light, but his ring was later given by Welles's son to a Cheltenham lawyer named John Bubb, whose trustees gave it to the Museum in 1947.

*Dr Edward Jenner's pen? (© Jenner Museum, Berkeley)*

Right *Edward Jenner, an engraving by Edward Scriven, after a painting by John Raphael Smith, about 1800.*

ONE OF CHELTENHAM'S most notable residents during the late eighteenth and early nineteenth century was Dr Edward Jenner (1749-1823), the pioneer of vaccination. Jenner either rented or owned a house in Cheltenham from 1795 onwards, initially in the High Street, but from 1796 to 1820 (in which year he finally retired to his birthplace, Berkeley), in St George's Place.

Sadly, Jenner's house was demolished in 1967 and replaced by a small car park, but it was rebuilt in replica in 1994-1995, following which a Civic Society plaque, recording his residence in the previous house, was affixed to the building.

In 1943, the Museum was given this ivory pen by Miss C.G. Burton of Cheltenham; unfortunately, the only document in its history file is a letter from the Curator thanking her for the gift of 'Dr Jenner's pen' – without any evidence to prove that it had indeed belonged to Jenner. It is, however, of the correct date, for the steel nib is stamped 'Beilby & Knott's Improved', Beilby & Knott being recorded in Birmingham directories as booksellers and stationers between 1818 and 1823.

*The Williams's Library weighing chair.*

DURING THE LATE eighteenth and nineteenth century, Cheltenham had a number of privately-owned circulating libraries, at which subscribers could read books and newspapers. The largest of these was that founded in 1815 by George Arthur Williams (1795-1880), which occupied part of the Assembly Rooms, at the corner of High Street and Rodney Road, between 1816 and its closure in 1896.

An additional attraction at the Library was its 'weighing chair', in which subscribers could be weighed, and then issued with a ticket stating their weight. When the Library closed, the chair, along with two weights, was presented to the Borough Council, and was probably stored in the Public Library until the opening of the Museum in 1907. The 'weighing book' and a number of early subscription books were also donated, and these are now in Gloucestershire Archives; although no example of a 'weighing ticket' has ever come to light, the engraved copper plate from which they were printed was given to the Museum in 1926.

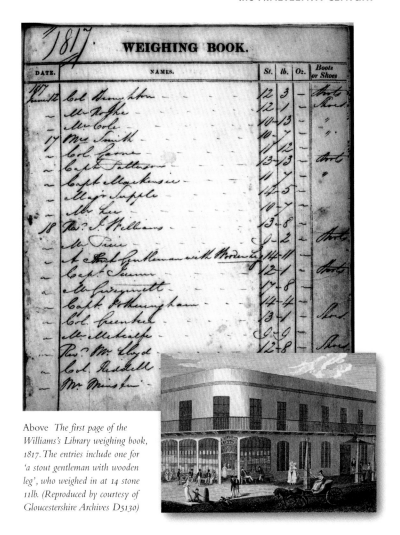

Above *The first page of the Williams's Library weighing book, 1817. The entries include one for 'a stout gentleman with wooden leg', who weighed in at 14 stone 11lb. (Reproduced by courtesy of Gloucestershire Archives D5130)*

Right *Williams's Library, an engraving published by G. A. Williams in his* New Guide to Cheltenham, *1824. Its site is now occupied by the High Street branch of Lloyds Bank.*

DURING THE NINETEENTH CENTURY, Cheltenham became a favoured place of residence for retired army and navy officers, many of whom had served in India and other parts of the Empire – so much so that in 1904, in his book *Cotswold and Vale*, Henry Branch would describe the town as 'the Anglo-Indian's Paradise'.

One such resident was Captain James Shrubb Iredell (1793-1872), who is known to have visited Cheltenham to 'take the waters' in the 1820s and who lived in the town from at least 1832 onwards. In 1840, he was one of a group of army officers and clergy who were responsible for establishing Cheltenham College, at which the sons of gentlemen (including his own) would receive an education based upon Anglican principles that would equip them for military or professional careers. Iredell served as the College's first Registrar and remained one of its Directors until 1862.

In 1985, five of Iredell's Australian great-grandchildren gave the Museum this jacket, complete with a pair of silver epaulettes in their original box. It dates from his time in the 15th Regiment of the Bombay Native Infantry, in which he served between 1808 and 1828.

*Captain James Shrubb Iredell's military jacket.*

*Captain Iredell, a watercolour by J. Thomas.
(Reproduced by permission of Cheltenham
College Archives; image courtesy of
Chorley's)*

*Cheltenham College, a steel engraving, 1844. The College opened in temporary premises in St George's Road in 1841, but moved to this new building in Bath Road in 1843.*

*Lady Russell's Indian beetlewing dress.*

CHELTENHAM'S ANGLO-INDIAN CONNECTIONS are also represented by this superb evening dress, which is believed to date from the late 1820s, and is said to have been worn at a ball in Calcutta by Jane Russell (*née* Sherwood, 1797-1888), a Major-General's daughter who married Dr (later Sir) William Russell, a prominent doctor in Calcutta. The couple returned to England in 1831 and in 1839 they took up residence at Charlton Park, in Charlton Kings, which Lady Jane had inherited in that year. After Sir William's death, also in 1839, Lady Russell continued to live at Charlton Park until 1851, but chose

to call herself Lady Prinn, after the family from whom she had inherited the property.

The dress is made of white Indian muslin, and is decorated with silver thread and more than 3,000 iridescent bluish-green beetle wing cases, each of which was individually sewn on by hand. In the photograph it is seen being worn at a fancy dress party by Lady Russell's great-granddaughter, Mrs Margot Arnold, who gave the dress to the Museum in 1943.

*A Chinese 'export' or 'trade' painting showing Oriel Lodge.*

NINETEENTH-CENTURY CHELTENHAM'S IMPERIAL connections also extended to China, where this oil painting of Oriel Lodge, one of the town's earliest Gothic Revival houses, is believed to have been produced sometime after 1824, the year in which the house was completed. That this very English scene is the work of a Chinese artist is suggested by the typically Chinese way in which the canvas is 'strained' on a traditional Chinese wooden support, and by its original carved and gilded Chinese frame.

Many Europeans commissioned paintings from Cantonese artists from the late eighteenth century onwards, but these were generally of Chinese scenes, and to find a Chinese painting of an English house is most unusual. The painting was almost certainly commissioned by the builder of the house, Captain Charles Sheldon Timins (1773-1838), a naval officer in the service of the East India Company, who is known to have spent some time in China. It was presumably based on a print or drawing sent (or taken) out to China, and there is indeed an almost identical lithograph of the house, by William Gauci, in Gloucestershire Archives.

Oriel Lodge, where Timins died in 1838, was one of the many villas built in the Montpellier estate during the early nineteenth century, and still exists, in Oriel Road, where it is now used as offices.

THE BANKER THOMAS COUTTS (1735–1822) – said to have been the richest untitled commoner in England by the time of his death – was one of the many prominent individuals who visited Cheltenham during the late eighteenth and early nineteenth century. In 1815, he married his second wife, the thirty-eight-year-old actress Harriot Mellon, whose stepfather, Thomas Entwisle, had opened a 'Musical Warehouse and Library' at Cheltenham in about 1802, and who served as the town's postmaster between 1805 and 1816.

Many items of Thomas Coutts's clothing were eventually given by a descendant to the Victoria & Albert Museum, which later distributed some of them to a number of other museums in Britain, Canada and the USA. These included, in 1934, Cheltenham Museum, which received this woollen tailcoat, which has been dated to some time after 1810, along with a waistcoat, an under-waistcoat, two pairs of breeches, a shirt, a pair of stockings and a knitted night cap.

*Thomas Coutts's coat.*

*Thomas Coutts, an engraving by Robert Sievier, published in 1822, after a portrait by Sir William Beechey. (© National Portrait Gallery, London)*

AMONG THE MANY charitable institutions that were established in Cheltenham during the early nineteenth century was the Female Orphan Asylum & School of Industry, which was founded in 1806, under the patronage of Queen Charlotte. Initially occupying a thatched barn in Wellington Passage, a lane off the north side of the High Street, it moved to a purpose-built asylum in Winchcombe Street in 1820, which was itself replaced by a new building, on the same site, in 1833.

The asylum, which was funded by voluntary subscriptions and regular fund-raising events, housed girls between the ages of eight and fifteen, and taught them the skills required to work as under-servants. These included sewing, and this pincushion (both sides of which are shown) is an example of the work that the girls would have undertaken during their training. They also spent some of their time making up cotton clothing, which was then sold to raise additional funds.

*A pin cushion from the Female Orphan Asylum & School of Industry.*

As well as this pincushion, the Museum also has a needlework 'sampler' that was worked at the asylum and a large wooden board, bearing the Royal coat of arms, which once hung in its entrance hall. The board was purchased by the Museum in 1958, the year in which the building was closed and demolished.

*The Female Orphan Asylum and entrance to Pittville, a lithograph published in about 1836.*

*Henry Lamb's* Cheltenhamorama.

THIS UNUSUAL CARD 'peep show', showing the Well Walk, was published by a Worcester-born artist named Henry Lamb (1799-1877), who worked in Cheltenham as a drawing master and topographical print maker between about 1819 and 1834.

By 1824 Lamb had opened a 'Repository of Arts' in the High Street, at which prints, artists' materials and souvenirs could be purchased, and within a year he had opened a second shop at the old or original spa well, which was usually known as the Royal Well after 1788.

The peep show, of which the Museum has two examples, is hand-coloured and shows a view looking north along the tree-lined Well Walk from its southern end, with the spa well in the centre and St Mary's Church in the distance. When flat, its front is decorated with a curious hand-coloured cave or grotto (which is painted differently in the two examples), through which the scene may be viewed when the whole thing is opened out like a concertina. It is contained in a cardboard sleeve, on which is pasted a label with its publication details, and the price of 7s 6d. The upper photograph on the opposite page shows these two features.

The Royal Wells, Cheltenham or Spasmodic affections from Spa Waters, *an engraving by Robert Cruikshank, 1825, showing Henry Lamb's 'Repository of Arts'.*

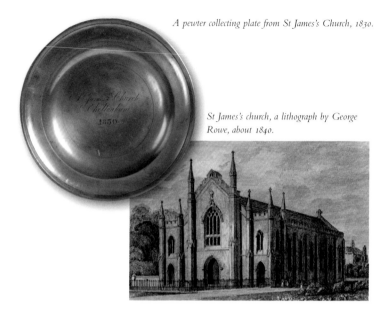

*A pewter collecting plate from St James's Church, 1830.*

*St James's church, a lithograph by George Rowe, about 1840.*

BETWEEN 1820 AND 1840, five new Anglican churches were built in Cheltenham as 'chapels of ease' to the parish church of St Mary, in order to cater for the town's rapidly growing population – and to counter the influence of the Nonconformists, who had opened a number of new chapels in the town since 1809.

One of these new churches was St James, in Suffolk Square, which was built in 1825-1830 to serve the fashionable population of both the Square itself and the adjoining Montpellier and Lansdown estates. Originally designed in the 'Regency Gothic' style by a local architect named Edward Jenkins, it was completed under the supervision of a London architect, John Papworth, after Jenkins had encountered technical difficulties with the spanning of the roof.

St James's became a parish church in its own right in 1916, but in 1972 it became a parish hall for St Philip & St James, Leckhampton and, more recently, in 2002, an Italian restaurant.

Shown above is one of a pair of the church's pewter collecting plates, bearing the date 1830, that were given to the Museum in 1936.

*A porcelain cake stand with a view of the Montpellier Spa.*

DURING THE FIRST half of the nineteenth century, a number of new spa wells were opened in the fields around the town, each with its own pump room, rivalling the Royal Well.

One of the most important of these was the Montpellier Spa, which was established by a London financier named Henry Thompson, who had purchased a large tract of land to the south of the town in 1801. From about 1804 onwards the spa waters were available at Hygeia House (later renamed Vittoria House, and still surviving in Vittoria Walk), which Thompson later made his own home, until in 1809 the first, wooden, spa building was constructed. This was replaced in 1817-1826 by the present stone building, which is often known as the Montpellier Rotunda because of its imposing dome, designed by John Papworth. Later used as a concert and dance hall, the building is now the Montpellier branch of Lloyds Bank.

This elaborate Chamberlain's Worcester cake stand, with its encrusted ceramic flowers, is one of the finest examples of souvenir ceramics in the Museum's collection. It shows the Montpellier Spa from the south, with the spire of St Mary's Church in the distance. It probably dates from about 1830.

*A marble sign advertising a Musical Promenade at Montpellier.*

Montpellier Promenade, *a lithograph by George Rowe, 1834, showing the visitors and the band of musicians, who are stationed under the colonnade of the Long Room. This print was published by Henry Davies, who ran the Montpellier Library in the building at right-angles to the Long Room between 1829 and 1848, in which year he moved his business to nearby Montpellier Street. During the 1830s and '40s, the trees of the walk were gradually cut down to make way for the shops of Montpellier Walk, with their unusual caryatids.*

IN ADDITION TO drinking the waters at the Rotunda, subscribers to the Montpellier Spa could 'promenade' in the adjoining walks, rides and gardens, often to the accompaniment of a band of musicians.

This thirty-two inch wide marble sign advertising an evening musical promenade at Montpellier was presumably once displayed somewhere close to the Rotunda, although exactly where is unknown. Also unknown is when it was taken down, but according to a note in the Museum Accessions Register, the family of the donor in 1974, Mrs Thompson of Parish School House, Knapp Lane, 'had it for some 50 years and it has been used as a table top'.

*A card model of the Pittville Pump Room by John Bellamy, 1835.*

THE MOST AMBITIOUS of Cheltenham's new spas was at Pittville, a 100-acre residential estate, set amidst gardens and tree-lined avenues, that was established on the north side of the town by a lawyer and banker named Joseph Pitt from 1824 onwards. Its focus was the Pittville Pump Room, which opened in 1830.

This card model of the Pump Room was made by John Bellamy (1808-1893), a Gloucestershire-born model-maker and travelling showman. On 25 May 1835, the *Cheltenham Journal* reported that 'a model of this spacious and magnificent structure has been completed by Mr Bellamy, an artist of great ability and rising celebrity, who is now engaged in preparing, on a similar scale, an exhibition of the principal buildings throughout the kingdom…the model has elicited the unqualified approbation of the numerous fashionable families by whom the Pump Room is…frequented and is entitled to the very highest commendation'.

During 1836-1837 this model, along with six others, was successively displayed at the Literary & Philosophical Institution in the Promenade, in an empty shop at Montpellier, and at the Pittville Pump Room itself. Bellamy later added many more models to his collection and toured the country with them for over forty years from 1837 onwards.

Although Bellamy sold most of his models in about 1878, he retained the Pump Room model and included it in a smaller collection with which he was travelling at the time of his death. Thereafter it passed to his daughter, and was eventually sold to the Museum by a descendant of her second husband in 1983.

THE REVEREND FRANCIS CLOSE (1797-1882) was one of the most influential figures in nineteenth-century Cheltenham. Appointed curate of Holy Trinity Church in 1824, he became incumbent of St Mary's, the parish church, two years later. He held that position for thirty years, until his appointment as Dean of Carlisle in 1856. Four years after his death, Dean Close School was founded in his memory.

A staunch Evangelical, Close was instrumental in the establishment of many of the town's new churches, schools, colleges and charities, and was a strong opponent of horse racing, the theatre, tobacco, alcohol and the running of trains on Sundays. He also disapproved of Nonconformity, Roman Catholicism and High Church Anglicanism. His influence was such that Alfred, Lord Tennyson, who often stayed in Cheltenham during the 1840s, described the town, somewhat ironically, as 'a place of which Francis Close is Pope'.

This plaster bust of Close is, unfortunately, anonymous, but one possible candidate for its maker is James Philip Papera, who is recorded as living in Cheltenham at various times between 1842 and his death in 1886. In 1847 he advertised himself as 'the celebrated statuary and modellist', who could supply 'Busts, in a superior style of Art, Five guineas Each'.

*A plaster bust of the Reverend Francis Close.*

The Reverend Francis Close, *a lithograph published by the Gloucester-born engraver George F. Bonner, who is recorded as living in Cheltenham in 1851. (© National Portrait Gallery, London)*

*A ceramic jar from Thomas Joslin, chemist and druggist, High Street.*

*Thomas Joslin's shop and its adjoining premises in the High Street, from George Rowe's* Illustrated Cheltenham Guide, *1845. Note the pestle & mortar trade sign.*

THIS CERAMIC JAR once contained 'Burman's Extract of Honey & Roses for the Hair', which, according to the printed text on the jar, was 'manufactured solely for the proprietor', Thomas Joslin of 371 High Street. The text claimed that 'the advantages and desiderata it possesses are those of preventing the Hair falling off, removing scurf (however firmly rooted), rendering the hair strong and of fine appearance, at the same time confering [*sic*] a most delightful odour'.

Joslin, who described himself as 'from Savory, Moore & Co.', a leading London chemist, advertised himself as 'Chemist to their Royal Highnesses the Duchess of Kent and the Princess Victoria'. Exactly when that honour was conferred is not known, but perhaps the Duchess and her daughter patronised the shop on 14 August 1830, during their afternoon tour of Cheltenham in the company of the then Master of the Ceremonies, Charles Marshall.

*One of a pair of duelling pistols by William Hollis, gunsmith, High Street.*

IN ABOUT 1815, William Sydney Hollis (1798-1867), a member of a well-established firm of Birmingham gun makers, moved to Cheltenham and established the Cheltenham Gun Manufactory at 89 High Street, by one of the entrances to St Mary's churchyard. Hollis continued to trade there until his retirement in 1858, when the business was taken over by an Irish gun maker named Charles McLoughlin, who ran it for the next thirty years.

Gradually, a number of other gun makers opened premises in the town, notably Tewkesbury-born Edwinson Charles Green, who had premises in the High Street from about 1870 onwards and whose firm continued trading in the town until about 1963.

This duelling pistol, which would have been one of a pair, has an inscription naming Hollis as 'maker to His Majesty', which would imply that it dates from before the accession of Queen Victoria in 1837.

*William Hollis's shop in the High Street, from Rowe's Illustrated Cheltenham Guide, 1845. The premises are still recognisable today.*

*Lord Ellenborough's personal seal.*

EDWARD LAW, 2nd Baron and 1st Earl of Ellenborough (1790-1871) was a prominent figure in the social and political life of early nineteenth-century Cheltenham. He lived from 1833 onwards at Southam de la Bere (now the Ellenborough Park Hotel), a large mansion in the village of Southam, between Cheltenham and Winchcombe.

Ellenborough occupied a number of important government positions under successive Tory administrations, including Lord Privy Seal, First Lord of the Admiralty, President of the Board of Control for India, and, between 1842 and 1844, Governor-General of India, from which post he was recalled early because of what the Directors of the East India Company regarded as his arrogant and high-handed behaviour.

One of the most exquisite items in the Museum's collections is Lord Ellenborough's personal seal, which was given to the Museum by the executors of one of his descendants in 1927. The seal, which is four inches long, is inlaid with gold and enamel, in an elaborate floral pattern. The actual 'seal imprint' is in the form of Hindu characters, which suggests that he might have acquired the seal while in India. It is contained in its original box, which is inlaid with a geometrical pattern of ivory and different woods.

*Lord Ellenborough, a watercolour by Richard Dighton, who lived and worked in Cheltenham in 1828 and again between 1832 and 1847.*

*A ticket and two examples of a white metal medal from the 1838 Centenary Fête.*

ON 8 AUGUST 1838, Cheltenham celebrated the hundredth anniversary of Henry Skillicorne's arrival in the town with a Public Breakfast and an Evening Gala Fête, both of which were held at the Royal Well. Both events were organised by the 'Town Committee for Entertainments', one of whose members, the artist and lithographer George Rowe, designed this admission ticket to the Public Breakfast (which cost 7s to attend), with a view of the Well and Well Walk. He also designed a white metal medal to mark the occasion, with a similar view and a suitable inscription; in April 1839, a specially produced gold version of the medal was presented to Queen Victoria.

The event was so successful that it was repeated annually at one or other of the spas, as the Anniversary Fête, until at least 1846. The Museum has an admission ticket for the 1839 Fête at the Montpellier Spa, which was also designed by George Rowe.

The Well Walk on the night of the Centenary Fête, *a lithograph by George Rowe, 1838.*

ALTHOUGH NINETEENTH-CENTURY CHELTENHAM was not primarily a manufacturing town, it did have a number of important local industries, including furniture making. One leading firm in this area was that of John Urch and William Seabright, which was established in 1826 in Gloucester Place, Fairview, an artisan area that was developed north of Albion Street from about 1807 onwards.

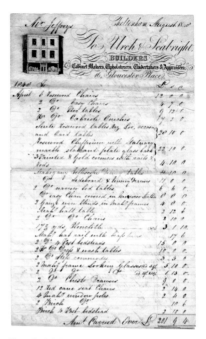

*Part of a bill for furniture from Urch & Seabright, cabinet makers and builders, Fairview, 1848.*

Urch & Seabright gradually expanded their business to become undertakers, builders and house agents, and in 1835 they purchased a large tract of land to the north of Fairview Road. There they either built, or sold for building, plots for thirty houses in Victoria Street (now part of Fairview Road), Victoria Place, Providence Square and School Lane. They also established a large timber yard and workshops in School Lane. The 1851 census – in which Urch & Seabright are recorded as employing fifty men – reveals that the occupants of many of these houses were employed in the woodworking trades.

After 1836 their Gloucester Place premises became a showroom, and in 1865 they opened a second showroom in a far more fashionable location at 11a Promenade Villas. By then, Seabright, who was thirteen years older than Urch, had retired and his son, William junior, had taken his place in the partnership, which continued until 1869. Thereafter, both William Seabright junior and Urch's two sons worked independently in a similar range of businesses for some years.

This invoice for furniture and carpeting, only part of which has survived, was issued to a Mr Jeffreys in August 1848. The bill head includes an attractive view of the firm's Gloucester Place showroom.

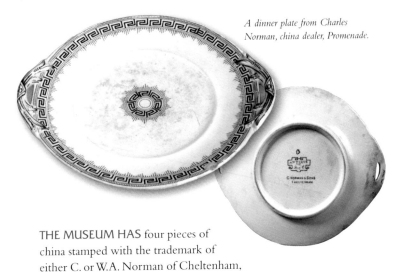

*A dinner plate from Charles Norman, china dealer, Promenade.*

THE MUSEUM HAS four pieces of china stamped with the trademark of either C. or W.A. Norman of Cheltenham, including this Staffordshire-made dinner plate with a blue 'Greek key' design, which probably dates from around 1840.

Although the firm's late nineteenth-century headed notepaper claimed that it was established in 1802, the earliest evidence for its existence is in 1827, when it is recorded as trading with the Wedgwood factory in Staffordshire. By 1839 it had a large showroom at 9 Promenade Villas, at the corner of Ormond Place, a site now occupied by Beards the jewellers. Its proprietor was Charles Norman (1799-1866), who was later succeeded by his son, William Austin Norman (1831-1909). In about 1876 he moved the business to Chelsea House, at the corner of Clarence Street and St George's Place, and later transferred the name to a new shop at the corner of Clarence Street and Well Walk (now Bank House) where he also sold antiques and traded as 'Norman's Emporium of Antiquities'. The business closed in about 1930.

*Charles Norman's china shop in the Promenade, from Rowe's* Illustrated Cheltenham Guide, *1845, in which the shop's stock was described as 'of the most chaste, classical and fashionable description'.*

*A pair of shoes from W. & T. Slade, shoemakers, Promenade.*

A BUSINESS THAT operated in the Promenade for more than 120 years was Slade's shoe shop, which opened in 1846 as a branch of a Worcester shoemaker that dated back to the late eighteenth century. Slade's traded at Imperial House, 12 Promenade Villas (later 78 Promenade), in premises that had previously been occupied by a haberdasher. In about 1930 they took over an adjoining shop and gradually diversified into hosiery and menswear. Slade's also had a branch at Great Malvern, and in 1920 they opened a fourth shop, in Cardiff.

This pair of blue kid shoes dates from soon after the opening of their Cheltenham shop. One of the shoes still retains its original trade label, which records the firm as 'boot shoe & clog makers' to Queen Adelaide, the widow of King William IV, to her sister Ida, Duchess of Saxe-Weimar, and to other female members of their family. The Dowager Queen, who died in 1849, lived at Witley Court in Worcestershire from 1842-1846, at which time Slade's designed 'a new and improved clog' for her, which they then marketed in their shops.

When Slade's finally closed in 1971, the Museum acquired many of its fittings, including a painted wooden crown stating that they traded 'By appointment to Her late Majesty Queen Adelaide', several doors with glass panels advertising the firm, many invoices and further examples of their shoes and shoeboxes.

53

THIS UNUSUAL ZINC chimney sweep's trade sign formerly hung outside 43 Sherborne Street, Fairview. It was sold to the Museum by Frederick Field, the last in a succession of sweeps to live at that address, following his retirement in 1950. It shows a master chimney sweep in his frock coat, bow tie and top hat; it was always known to the Field family as 'the old man'.

A number of sweeps are recorded in Sherborne Street from 1825 onwards, beginning with John Russell, whose widow, Ann, took over after his death in 1843. She soon married a Bristol-born sweep, James Short, with whom she ran the business until his death in 1869. It

*A zinc chimney sweep's trade sign from Sherborne Street, Fairview.*

was the Shorts who first lived at No. 43, and the trade sign may date from their time.

One of Short's 'climbing boys' was William Field, the son of a Charlton Kings shoemaker, who took over the business following Ann Short's death in 1870. He ran it until his death in 1901, when his thirty-year-old son, Frederick, took over. At the time of Fred's retirement, forty-nine years later, he was said to have been the country's oldest working chimney sweep.

In addition to the sign, the Museum also has the brass plate from the front door of 43 Sherborne Street, advertising 'Wm Field (late J. Short) chimney sweeper' and a set of chimney sweeping brushes, both given by Fred Field's son, Arthur, in 1980.

*Fred Field and his wife Agnes outside 43 Sherborne Street on the day of Fred's retirement in August 1950, photographed by Eric Franks ARPS. (Reproduced by courtesy of Jim Stevenson)*

IN 1822, a Bath jeweller named Samuel Martin opened a branch establishment in Cheltenham High Street. In 1833 the shop moved to its current premises at Imperial Circus at the southern end of the Colonnade, and in 1838 the firm was appointed 'goldsmiths in ordinary' to Queen Victoria. By then it traded as Martin & Baskett.

This claret jug, in the 'Italian Renaissance style' that was fashionable in the mid-nineteenth century, was produced by Martins as part of their display of plate at the Great Exhibition of 1851. It stands just under twelve inches

*A silver claret jug from Martin, Baskett & Martin, jewellers and watchmakers, Imperial Circus, 1851.*

high and is made of silver with ivory mounts to its handle and a silver-gilt lid. Its hallmark bears the letters CR/GS, which probably refers to one of two London silversmiths, Reily & Storer, or Rawlins & Sumner.

The Museum also has a bracket clock retailed by Martins and a large enamel sign advertising the firm and its branches at Southsea and Liverpool.

*Martins's shop, from Rowe's Illustrated Cheltenham Guide, 1845. This is the only business shown in Rowe's Guide that is still located in the same premises today. Note the Royal coat of arms on the exterior of the shop.*

*A ceramic tray showing the Cheltenham Crystal Palace, 1854.*

DURING THE EARLY 1850s, a number of major floral and horticultural exhibitions were held in the grounds of the Royal Well
including, between 1 June and 12 July 1854, the 'Cheltenham
Great Exhibition of Horticulture and of Works of Art and Design
Connected Therewith'. The exhibition's 'centrepiece' was a specially
designed 'Crystal Palace', constructed by a local builder (and later
Mayor of Cheltenham), George Parsonage, and then demolished
after the exhibition had ended. Five fountains were installed in the
grounds and the Royal Well building itself was turned into a Museum
of Curiosities. Among local exhibitors were Martin, Baskett & Martin,
and Charles Norman, who had displays of plate and china respectively.

This ceramic tray, which was manufactured by William Davenport
& Company of Stoke-on-Trent, shows the short-lived 'Crystal Palace'.

*The trowel used at the laying of the foundation stone of the New Chapel, Bays Hill, 1864.*

MANY NONCONFORMIST CHAPELS were built in Cheltenham during the nineteenth century, including a United Methodist (later Association Methodist) chapel on the north side of St George's Road, opposite the entrance to Cheltenham Ladies' College.

Designed by local architect C.M. Muller, the chapel's foundation stone was laid on 24 June 1864 by William Nash Skillicorne, the great-grandson of Henry Skillicorne, the 'founding father' of the spa.

In his speech, Skillicorne remarked that 'the handsome trowel and mallet now presented to him he should present to his son, to be handed down as heirlooms in the family'; unfortunately, whoever engraved the trowel omitted the final 'e' from Skillicorne's surname and one wonders if he had noticed the spelling mistake! Although the mallet has never come to light, the trowel was given to the Museum in 1952.

The chapel, often known as the Royal Well Chapel, was opened on 8 March 1866 and eventually closed in 1936, after which it became a garage, Belle Vue Motors. It was demolished to make way for a small car park in 1965.

The Museum has four other trowels that were used for similar occasions – for the turning of the first sod of the Dowdeswell Reservoir (1883), the laying of the foundation stone of the Public Library and Schools of Art & Science (1887), the opening of a new tank at the gasworks (1887), and the opening of Gloucester Road Schools (1906).

*A pencil drawing of the former chapel, by Philip Smith, 1952. (Reproduced by permission of the artist's estate)*

*William Nash Skillicorne (1807-1887). From 1861 until his death, Skillicorne was Chairman of the Cheltenham Bench of Magistrates, and served as the town's first Mayor following its incorporation as a Borough in 1876, and again in 1879.*

*The North Place Chapel pipe organ, 1865.*

Below *North Place Chapel, from Rowe's* Illustrated Cheltenham Guide, *1845. A porch was added to building in 1865, the same year in which the organ was built.*

EACH OF THE town's major churches and chapels had a pipe organ, the earliest of which to survive being from the former North Place Chapel (now Chapel Spa health centre), which was built in 1816 and occupied from 1819 onwards by the Countess of Huntingdon's Connection.

In 1865, an organ builder named Henry Williams, who had trained in London before establishing a workshop adjoining Handel House in St George's Place in 1853, provided the chapel with a fine new organ. This remained in use until the late 1980s, when it was dismantled prior to major building work on the chapel. This photograph, by the late Harold Cheesman, was taken shortly before it was dismantled.

Unfortunately, by 1990 it had become clear that the congregation would be unable to retain the building, and that new homes would need to be found for its fittings, including the organ. Fortunately, the Summerfield Charitable Trust agreed to fund the Museum's purchase of the organ in January 1991 and its temporary removal to St Luke's Church, where it was hoped to raise sufficient funds to reassemble and use it until such time as it could be displayed at the Museum. Those funds were not, however, forthcoming, and in November 1992 the organ was moved to the Museum's out-store, where it still remains.

*Two items of Mauchline Ware showing St Mary's Hall.*

MANY WOODEN, as well as ceramic, souvenirs of Cheltenham were produced during the nineteenth century, almost always with transfer-printed views of the town. Virtually all of them were made in Scotland, notably in the Ayrshire town of Mauchline, which has given its name to this type of product, which is also sometimes known as Scottish Souvenir Ware.

These two examples – an egg cup and a thimble holder – are part of a large collection of Mauchline Ware with views of Cheltenham that was given to the Museum by local collector John Baker in 1992. They are made of sycamore, and both show St Mary's Hall, which was built in 1869 as the female department of St Paul's teacher training college. The new building replaced the Old Farm at the corner of St George's Place and Manchester Street (now part of Clarence Street), which had been the home of the Skillicorne family since the 1730s.

Later renamed Shaftesbury Hall, the building was sold by the College (which is now the Francis Close campus of the University of Gloucestershire) in 1994 and now forms part of the Chelsea Square housing development.

*Two black lacquered wooden souvenirs showing the Winter Garden.*

SCOTTISH SOUVENIR WARE also included items of fern ware, tartan ware and black lacquered ware. These two items – a trinket box and a letter opener – are examples of the latter and show the large Winter Garden that was built in Imperial Square by a private company in 1878. The building was intended as a venue for concerts, exhibitions and roller skating, and also served as a cinema between 1912 and 1939.

By 1895 the building's owners were in financial difficulties, and its future was uncertain, so the Borough Council stepped in and purchased it; eight years later, in 1903, the Town Hall was opened to one side of it as an additional venue for the town following the demolition of the Assembly Rooms in 1900.

During the early twentieth century, the Winter Garden was often seen as something of a 'white elephant', as it needed constant, and often costly, repair. Many ratepayers were probably not unhappy to see it dismantled from 1940 onwards, ostensibly so that its glass roof would not attract enemy aircraft!

*A ceramic pie dish from George's, bakers and confectioners, High Street.*

Right *George's High Street premises, from* The Garden Town of England, *1901.*

ACCORDING TO ITS own publicity, the prominent Cheltenham baker, confectioner and caterer, George's, was established in 1800, although the earliest directory reference to the firm is in 1830, when David George (1801-1848), a baker and pastry cook, was recorded at 3-4 Arcade, a row of shops now represented by Bennington Street.

By 1838 the business had moved to 367 High Street, a little to the east of the Promenade, where it remained until its closure in 1940. George's later expanded into an adjoining shop, opened a restaurant, and ran a successful outside catering business. By 1890 it had opened at least five other shops in the town, plus a 'tuck shop' at Cheltenham College and branches at Malvern, Worcester and Weston-super-Mare. Among its best-known products were its 'bride cakes' and its 'Royal Cheltenham Ice Wafers', which were regularly supplied to the Royal Household.

One of the company's new shops, opened in 1889, was at 4 Bedford Buildings (now 51 Clarence Street), which is now part of the Art Gallery & Museum's premises; adjoining it was a model bakery, the site of which is now occupied by part of the 2013 Museum extension.

This dish, which measures just over seven inches across, probably pre-dates 1888, when George's became a Limited Company. It once contained a meat (or possibly fish or fruit) pie, to which the sum of 4*d* was added, to be redeemed when the dish was returned to the shop.

DR EDWARD ADRIAN WILSON (1872–1912), an accomplished artist, doctor, naturalist and scientist, was born at 6 (now 91) Montpellier Terrace, the son of a Cheltenham physician, Dr Edward Thomas Wilson. He attended Cheltenham College between 1886 and 1891, before going up to Cambridge to read natural sciences. He later served as an artist and scientific officer on Captain Scott's two Antarctic expeditions and died with Captain Scott and three of their companions on their return journey from the South Pole in March 1912.

*Dr Edward Wilson's christening mug, 1872.*

Soon after Wilson's death, members of his family, and others connected with him, began to donate to the Museum artefacts, paintings, documents, photographs and scientific specimens connected with his life and Antarctic journeys. This has continued ever since, most notably with the donation, by the Wilson family in 1995, of a large archive relating not only to the explorer, but also to other members of this prominent nineteenth- and early twentieth-century Cheltenham family. The Museum now has one of Britain's most important Antarctic collections, highlights of which include a watch and a compass that were found on Wilson's body and the prayer book used at the burial of Wilson, Scott and Bowers on the Great Ice Barrier in November 1912.

One of the most recent additions to the collection is this silver gilt christening mug, bearing Wilson's name and the date of his birth, 23 July 1872. It was given to the Museum by his great-nephew, Christopher Wilson, following a service held at Cheltenham College on 18 March 2012 to mark the centenary of Wilson's death.

*Edward Wilson as a baby, 1873, from one of his father's photograph albums.*

*An engraved copper plate and its original wrapper, advertising Edwin Beckingsale, ironmonger, High Street.*

A NUMBER OF tradesmen by the name of Beckingsale ran businesses in the town during the nineteenth century, including Edwin Beckingsale (1846-1929), who is recorded in local directories at 149 High Street, at the corner of Bennington Street, between 1872 and 1897.

In 1941, his son, Mr G.W. Beckingsale, gave the Museum an engraved copper plate advertising his father's business, which records that he was a 'General Ironmonger & Cutler, Gas Fitter, Bell Hanger, Brazier & Tinman' and that he supplied 'Burning Oils of best quality', Agricultural Implements and Water Apparatus, and that he undertook 'repairs of every description'. An account of his business in 1890 noted that one of the shop's specialities was 'Anglo-American cooking stoves' and that 'Mr Beckingsale never tires of demonstrating their peculiar advantages to intending customers'.

Coincidentally, more than fifty years later, in 1992, another member of the Beckingsale family gave the Museum what is almost certainly the paper wrapper in which the copper plate was originally contained, on which three impressions from the plate have been printed.

COACH BUILDERS ARE recorded as working in Cheltenham from as early as 1818. Among them was William Mills (1829-1915), whose workshops were established at 31-33 Mountpleasant, Winchcombe Street (close to its junction with Fairview Road) in 1860. By 1877 Mills had opened a showroom at 35 Winchcombe

*A Brougham Carriage by William Mills, coach builder, Winchcombe Street.*

Street and in the following year he took over the adjacent premises of another coach builder, Henry Arkell, at 38 Winchcombe Street. Mills was later joined in the business by his sons, and by 1913 the business had also become 'automobile engineers', which it remained until 1925, when it became the Cheltenham Car Mart.

In 1986, the Museum was given this fine Brougham Carriage, whose hub caps are stamped with Mills's name and his 35 and 38 Winchcombe Street addresses. The carriage was given by members of the Kennard family, who are descended from a Leeds industrialist named John Waddingham, who lived at Guiting Grange, a large house at Guiting Power in the Cotswolds, from 1842 onwards. The coach is believed to have been housed there until the Grange was demolished in 1971, at which time it was moved to a barn at nearby Barton Farm, from where it was eventually transferred to the Museum.

The photograph show the carriage before it was given to the Museum. It was later restored at the Bristol Industrial Museum with a grant from the Area Museum Council for the South West.

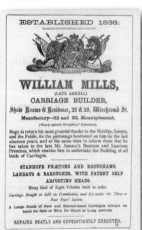

*An advertisement for William Mills's business, from the 1880 Cheltenham Post Office Directory; note the original spelling of 'Winchcomb', without the final 'e'. The date 1838 refers to the establishment of Henry Arkell's business. (Reproduced by courtesy of Cheltenham Local & Family History Centre)*

*A paper bag from W. Clarke & Co., grocers, Winchcombe Street.*

THIS PAPER BAG is one of the most unusual items in the Museum's collection of printed ephemera in that it was found as part of a 'time capsule' when the site of Clarke's shop, at the corner of Winchcombe Street and Warwick Place, was being excavated during the construction of Cheltenham's Northern Relief Road in 1984.

The bag, which was produced for Clarke by the leading Bristol paper bag manufacturers, E.S. & A. Robinson, has a fine view of Clarke's shop and details of his products. It was found rolled up in a ginger beer bottle from the local Bartholemew's Brewery, along with a hand-written card stating that 'this floor was laid 1903 by W. & H. Clarke'.

William Clarke (born 1846) was from Leonard Stanley, near Stroud, and is first recorded as a baker at 88 Albion Street in 1871. By 1873 he had taken over the premises shown on the bag, which had previously been those of another baker, J. Chambers. His business is recorded there until 1917, although it may have continued for a couple of years thereafter, as there are no further directories until 1922, in which year the premises were recorded as those of a corn merchant named J.T. Wyatt.

*A Royal coat of arms from Silk & Son, grocers & provision merchants, High Street.*

THIS CARVED WOODEN coat of arms is one of only two that have survived from those Cheltenham businesses that traded 'by Royal Appointment' during the nineteenth century; the other may still be seen outside John Dower House (once the Clarence Hotel) in Crescent Place.

Jacob Silk (1821–1896), from the Cotswold village of Miserden, opened a grocery business at 349 High Street, by one of the lanes leading to St Mary's churchyard, in 1842. By 1853 he had moved to larger premises, No. 146, on the opposite side of the High Street, by Rose & Crown Passage, and by 1872 he had opened a second shop at 430 High Street, to the east of Bath Road.

This coat of arms was once displayed above the door of 430 High Street, and is shown in the photograph on the opposite page, from the 1891-2 *Cheltenham & District Post Office Directory*; it is the only known photograph to show the sign *in situ*.

Although the photograph suggests that Silks traded 'By Appointment to H.R.H. The Prince of Wales', a puzzling note in the object's history file suggests that the coat of arms may already have been outside the shop when Silks took it over, and that they were eventually asked to remove it!

The lettering may still be seen on the building, which is now part of the Strand Bar. The sign was purchased by the Museum in 1932, and the firm is listed at 430 High Street in local directories until 1934, although it continued trading elsewhere in the town until the 1970s.

SILK & SON.

POST OFFICE

# SILK & SON,

## GROCERS & PROVISION MERCHANTS

### Dealers in Wines and Spirits,

## 4·3·0, H·I·G·H S·T·R·E·E·T,

### CHELTENHAM.

#### Agents for Kinloch's Catalan Wines.

*An advertisement board for the Cambray Spa Turkish Baths.*

THE OCTAGONAL CAMBRAY SPA, at the corner of Oriel Road and Rodney Road, was opened in 1834, with both saline and chalybeate (iron-rich) waters. It succeeded an earlier (1807) spa building, known as Fowler's Cottage (later renamed Woodland Villa, and now demolished), which stood a little further north.

In 1873, as a result of the declining popularity of the spas, William Ruck (1813–1886), a chiropodist and 'medical galvanist', who had previously managed the Montpellier Baths, converted the building into a Turkish bath, while still making the spa waters available to those who wished to take them. So it remained until 1938, when it was demolished to make way for a car park.

This water-stained advertisement board is believed to have been rescued from a rubbish tip on the site of the building in February 1938, and given to the Museum.

**CHELTENHAM'S EARLIEST RAILWAY STATION,** on the Midland Railway's proposed line from Bristol to Birmingham, opened at Lansdown in 1840 and is now the only one of the District's eventual seven stations and halts, on five separate lines, that is still is use.

*A leather cash bag, luggage label and four tickets from St James's railway station.*

On 23 October 1847, the Great Western Railway opened the town's second station on part of the former Jessop's Nurseries in St James's Square, thereby connecting the town with London, via Swindon. That station continued in use until the line's closure in 1966, since when its site has been redeveloped for office and retail premises, including the Waitrose store.

In 1985, a collection of railway material relating to Cheltenham (formerly part of the Roger Burdett Wilson collection of 'railwayana'), including these items from St James's station, were transferred to Cheltenham by the Bristol Industrial Museum. More recently, BIM has also transferred a jigsaw puzzle showing 'the Cheltenham Flyer', once the country's fastest train, which used to run on the London to Cheltenham line.

*A steam train at St James's Station, about 1910. In the background are the tower and spire of St Gregory's Roman Catholic Church and the spire of St Matthew's Church, which was taken down in 1952.*

ONE OF THE many notable sportsmen and women who are associated with Cheltenham is the champion archer, Alice Blanche Legh (1855-1948). Although never a resident of the town, she was a long-standing member of the Cheltenham Archery Club, and won the national ladies' championship twenty-three times between 1881 and 1922. She is arguably the greatest British woman archer of all time.

*An archery belt and score book belonging to the champion archer, Alice Legh.*

The Cheltenham Archers were founded in 1857, the year after a Grand National Archery Meeting had been held at Cheltenham College. Its founder, a solicitor named Horace Ford, had moved to Cheltenham in about 1855 and was himself a national champion, who was – according to a Civic Society plaque in Montpellier Gardens, where the club's target bosses were once a common sight – 'the father of modern archery changing a Victorian amusement into an Olympic sport'.

Although Alice Legh never competed in the Olympics, another member of the Cheltenham Archers did, namely Sybil 'Queenie' Newall, who won a gold medal in 1908, at the age of fifty-three, and remains the oldest woman ever to have done so.

In addition to this archery belt and score book, the Museum also has a bow and a box of arrows that once belonged to Alice Legh.

*Alice Legh, by an unknown photographer, about 1900.*

*A model of St Stephen's Church.*

BETWEEN 1840 AND 1880, as the town's population continued to grow, six new Anglican churches were built in Cheltenham, plus one each in Charlton Kings and Leckhampton.

Five of these new churches were designed by the architect John Middleton (1820-1885), who lived and worked in Cheltenham from 1860 onwards. One of them was St Stephen's, which was built to serve the area known as Tivoli, to the south of Montpellier. The earliest part of the building was the chancel, built in 1873-1874, with a north transept and nave built in 1876 and 1881-1883 respectively. The north and south porches were added in 1885 and 1886, but plans to add a tower and spire above the north porch were eventually abandoned in 1930.

This model of St Stephen's Church was 'discovered' on a shelf in the St Stephen's Club (formerly the Tivoli Institute) in Tivoli Street in 1972, transferred to the church itself in 1983, and given to the Museum in 1988. Although neither its maker nor its exact date are known, it appears to show the church as it would have looked following the building of its boundary wall in 1884, but before the addition of the north porch in 1885. Perhaps it was the work of someone who attended the Institute, which was founded in 1884, and formed something of a social centre for the parish until the 1920s.

*A wrought iron picture frame by William Letheren, art metalworker.*

DURING THE SECOND half of the nineteenth century, Cheltenham gained a considerable reputation for high-quality craftmanship in wood, stone and metal. One of the earliest notable craftsmen to work in these areas was the art metalworker William Letheren (1836-1910), who ran the Vulcan Iron Works, near Lansdown railway station, from about 1860 until 1907.

The Museum has a number of examples of Letheren's work, including this delicate wrought-iron picture frame (above, right), which is eight inches high. It contains a photograph of a small girl holding two kittens; unfortunately there is no indication of who she might be.

The Museum also has, on loan from the Victoria & Albert Museum, a forty-two-inch high 'trial piece' for an elaborate 'medieval style' ironwork screen which won Letheren a Society of Arts prize in 1867; a photograph of Letheren standing beside the full-size screen, the current whereabouts of which is unknown, is shown above.

## FREDERICK JAMES ARCHER

*A ceramic plate commemorating the jockey Fred Archer, 1886.*

(1857-1886) was one of Victorian England's most successful jockeys. He was the country's champion jockey for thirteen consecutive years, between 1874 and his death in 1886, and his record of 246 winners in a single year was not equalled until 1933.

Archer was the son of William Archer, a steeplechase rider, and was born in the small cottage off St George's Place that now bears a plaque recording his birth; an earlier plaque had been affixed to the house fronting St George's Place in 1919, but it was later removed when the error was realised! Soon after his birth, Archer's family moved to Prestbury, where his father became publican of the Kings Arms in 1861; it was at Prestbury that Archer first learnt to ride.

In 1868, his obvious talent led to his being apprenticed to one of the leading trainers of the day, Mathew Dawson at Newmarket, the town in which Archer later made his home. It was also there that, tragically, he took his own life on 8 November 1886, while suffering from a depression that was probably caused by a combination of typhoid fever and grief at the death of both his infant son and his wife (shortly after giving birth to a daughter) in 1884.

This octagonal plate is No. 58 in a series of 'portrait plates' depicting famous contemporaries that was produced by Wallis, Gimson & Co. of Lane Delph Pottery in Fenton (Staffordshire) between 1884 and 1889. Although this particular design was registered on 11 January 1886, it must have been produced later in the year, as Archer's 1886 winners are included, and it may even be posthumous. Unfortunately, both the number of his races (which should be 8,084) and the number of his wins (which should be 2,748) are incorrect!

The Museum also has a number of other 'souvenirs' of Archer's life, including paintings, prints, woven silk pictures and two examples of a clay pipe impressed with a portrait of Archer. In 2006, the Museum was given the plaque that had previously been attached to the wrong house in St George's Place.

APART FROM CAVENDISH HOUSE, which dates back to 1826, the earliest of the Promenade's clothing shops was that established in about 1833 by Alexander Shirer and Donald Macdougall. In 1838, they became 'mercers, lacemen and drapers in ordinary' to Queen Victoria, the original Royal warrant for which is now in the Museum collection.

The firm later diversified into carpets, furniture and funerals, and their premises eventually occupied most of the Colonnade, with frontages to both the Promenade and Clarence Street, as well as a large furniture warehouse at the corner of Clarence Street and Well Walk.

*A catalogue for Shirer & Haddon, outfitters, Imperial Circus and Clarence Street, 1888.*

After 1838 the firm's name changed a number of times, from Shirer & Co. in 1845 (following Macdougall's death) to Shirer & Sons in 1854 and Shirer, Son & Haddon in 1866, after another draper, John Haddon, had joined the business. Eventually, in about 1938, the firm combined with John Lance & Co. to become Shirer & Lance's, which it remained until its closure in 1979.

This catalogue of 1888 provides an insight into the firm's stock, and certainly confirms an 1890 account of its ladies' and children's departments as containing 'a magnificent display of every description of high-class goods, including silks, cashmeres, french merinos, cloths and other dress materials in every shade and texture, as well as hosiery, gloves, hats, bonnets, flowers, laces, feathers, trimmings, ribbons, fancy goods, millinery requisites and umbrellas'.

## LIEUTENANT-COLONEL NEWMAN BURFOOT THOYTS

**THOYTS** (1831–1918) was an Indian Army Officer who retired to Cheltenham in 1876 and soon became involved in local politics. He became a Conservative member of the Borough Council in 1885 and served three terms as Mayor between 1888 and 1891. In nominating him, his predecessor as Mayor, the draper John

*A pair of kid gauntlets presented to Mayor Newman Burfoot Thoyts, 1890.*

Haddon, described Thoyts as a man who 'moved in the best society in the town, and was respected alike in the military world and in civil life'.

In April 1890, a delegation of Councillors and Aldermen presented Thoyts with a pair of white kid gauntlets, with the Borough's coat of arms on the cuffs. Their design was based on surviving sixteenth-century gloves, and they were specially made by Messrs Bryant & Co., tailors and outfitters at 1 Colonnade.

In 1892, Thoyts presented the Council with a coloured photograph of himself in his Mayoral robes; that is almost certainly the

photograph shown below, which is one of a large collection of Mayoral photographs that have been transferred to the Museum from the Municipal Offices.

The gloves, along with their casket, which has Thoyts's monogram engraved on it, were given to the Museum by a descendant in 2001. They joined a similar pair of gauntlets that had been presented to Mayor George Parsonage in 1883, and which had been given to the Museum by his family in 1943.

*A 'Grand Xmas Bazaar' catalogue from Dicks and Sons, drapers, High Street.*

JAMES DICKS (1829-1903) established a hosiery and haberdasher's business at the corner of Lower High Street and the east side of St George's Street in 1871. In about 1880, the firm, known by then as Dicks & Sons, opened a branch shop in Great Norwood Street, and in about 1888 they took over and remodelled an old house on the opposite corner of St George's Street as a china and carpet shop. Their shops were regarded as less exclusive (and therefore less expensive) than those in the Promenade, and the firm was sometimes known as 'the people's draper', with the advertising motto 'good value, large assortment and popular prices'. Its local importance was such that the junction of Lower High Street and St George's Street and Square became known as 'Dicks's Corner'. The business eventually closed in about 1964.

This four-page broadsheet probably dates from the 1890s and advertises a wide range of potential Christmas gifts.

*Dicks & Sons's premises at the corners of Lower High Street and St George's Street, from* Where to Buy at Cheltenham, *a shopping guide published in 1890. (Reproduced by courtesy of Cheltenham Local & Family History Centre)*

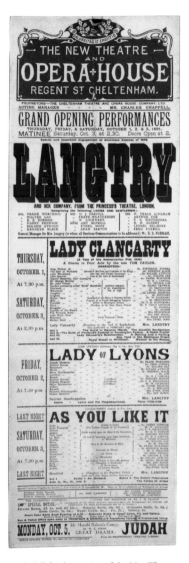

*A playbill for the opening of the New Theatre and Opera House, 1891.*

FOLLOWING THE DESTRUCTION of the Theatre Royal by fire in 1839, Cheltenham lacked a purpose-built theatre until the Royal Well Pump Room was rebuilt as a Theatre and Music Hall in 1849-1850. In 1890, that building was purchased by Cheltenham Ladies' College, which prompted a group of local people to establish a private company to build a new theatre for the town.

That ambition was realised on 1 October 1891, when the New Theatre and Opera House (now the Everyman Theatre) in Regent Street was opened with a performance by the actress Lillie Langtry and her company, as recorded in this playbill.

This is just one of a collection of over 3,000 playbills covering performances in the town's theatres and other entertainment venues since the 1780s that are held by the Museum, and which form a rich resource for the town's theatrical history.

THE COMPOSER GUSTAV HOLST (1874-1934) was born at 4 Pittville Terrace (now 4 Clarence Road), the son of Adolph von Holst, a musician and teacher of German descent, and his English wife, Clara Lediard. The young Holst showed an early aptitude for music, and began composing at the age of twelve, trying out his compositions on the organ at All Saints' Church, where his father was choirmaster and organist. Between 1886 and 1892, Holst was a pupil at Cheltenham Grammar School, before leaving Cheltenham, initially to be the organist at Wyck Rissington church, and then a student at the Royal College of Music.

*A manuscript score by Gustav Holst, 1891. (© Reproduced by permission of the Holst Foundation)*

From 1954 onwards, Holst's daughter, Imogen, donated many of her father's possessions to Cheltenham Art Gallery & Museum, including the piano on which he composed his most famous work, *The Planets*. Most of these are now on display at the Holst Birthplace Museum, which opened as a branch museum in 1975, but which is now run by an independent charitable trust.

Imogen Holst also donated a large collection of documents and photographs, including eight of Holst's early manuscript scores, dating from the years 1891-1893.

One of the early manuscripts was this four-page score for an organ voluntary, *Allegretto Pastorale*, dated 1891. It still remains unpublished, although there are plans to have it, and Holst's other early works, performed and recorded so that they may be heard by visitors to the Birthplace Museum's new 'Holst Discovery Space'.

*Gustav Holst while a student, about 1898.*

LIKE SO MANY towns, Cheltenham's earliest industries included brewing and malting, references to which date back to the seventeenth century. In 1760, John Gardner established what was to be the town's most important brewery, later known as the Original Brewery, which stood on the north side of the High Street. During the nineteenth century many smaller breweries also opened in the town, including the Albion Brewery in Gloucester Road and the Anchor Brewery in Winchcombe Street.

The Museum has a large collection of objects, prints, photographs and printed ephemera relating to the town's breweries, including this late nineteenth-century canvas bag containing fifty-four small brass tokens, which employees at the Original Brewery would receive as part of their wages, each of which could be exchanged for a pint of the company's beer.

*A canvas bag containing fifty-four beer tokens from the Cheltenham Original Brewery.*

*A billhead for Gardner's Original Brewery, about 1840, with an engraving by Jonas Radford showing a brewer's dray, piled with barrels, leaving the brewery premises.*

*An election card for Alton William Hillen, 1895.*

CHELTENHAM OBTAINED THE right to return its own Member of Parliament under the 1832 Reform Act, and the Museum has a large collection of printed ephemera relating to local elections from that time onwards.

This rather amusing election card from the 1895 General Election was issued by a solicitor named Alton William Hillen (1850–1917). Although born in Cheltenham, the son of a Fairview cabinet maker, Hillen appears to have spent most of his life away from the town and the only local directory in which he appears is 1896, when he is recorded at The Grange in Malvern Road.

Hillen stood as an Independent Conservative and according to the Conservative newspaper, the *Cheltenham Looker-On* for 13 July 1895, his candidature 'has scarcely been regarded as serious, though his address had been published for more than a week. In it no definite declaration of political party or principle has been made, and beyond the fact that he was a native of Cheltenham who had recently returned to the town there was nothing on which a claim to support could be based'. Clearly the electors agreed, for on election day, 15 July – at which he was not present – he polled just twenty-three votes!

Cartoons of Hillen and his two rivals are depicted on the card. On the left is Colonel Frank Shirley Russell, the official Conservative candidate, who won the election, while in the centre is Hillen himself, who seems to be 'seeing off' the Liberal candidate, another solicitor named Wilfred Blaydes.

*A Freedom Casket presented to James Tynte Agg-Gardner, 1896.*

THE BREWER JAMES TYNTE AGG-GARDNER (1846-1928), who was knighted in 1916, was a great benefactor to the town and served as its Conservative MP for a total of thirty-nine years between 1874 and 1928. He also served as the town's Mayor in 1908-1909 and 1912-1913.

In 1896, the Council voted to make him the town's first Honorary Freeman 'in recognition of his valuable services as Member for the Parliamentary Borough in Parliament for a period of sixteen years, of the part taken by him in the incorporation of the Municipal Borough, of his munificent gift to the Town of a public pleasure and recreation ground and of his generous and liberal support of its public institutions'.

On 30 October 1896, he was presented with this inscribed oak and silver casket, which contained the illuminated Freedom Certificate (which is shown opposite) and a book listing the 330 subscribers towards the gift. The casket is thirteen inches wide and was made by local jewellers, Messrs Furber, Son & Ellis, who entrusted the wood carving to H.H. Martyn & Company. It features both Agg-Gardner's and the Borough's coats of arms and is embellished with four enamel plaques showing St Mary's Church, Cheltenham College, the Grammar School and the Pittville Pump Room. Both the casket and its contents were eventually returned to the Council and transferred to the Museum.

The Council also commissioned an oil painting of Agg-Gardner from the artist Herman Herkomer, which was to hang in the Council Offices; the pen and ink drawing (shown above) is almost certainly Herkomer's original sketch for the painting, which has also now been transferred to the Museum.

*A match holder and striker incorporating a deer's foot, 1899.*

**THE ORIGINAL PLANS** for Cheltenham's Free Library and Schools of Art & Science, which opened in 1889, included to the east of the main building another structure to house 'Museum and Pictures'. Its proposed site remained vacant until 1899, when a single-storey art gallery was opened to house the collection of Dutch and other northern European paintings presented to the town by Baron de Ferrieres, who also gave £1,000 towards the cost of building the Gallery.

On 25 October 1899, the day before it opened to the public, an inauguration dinner, hosted by the Baron, was held in the new gallery, the menu for which included a haunch of venison donated by Major-General John Macdonald, a member of the Borough Council.

As a gift for the Baron, Macdonald commissioned the local jewellers, Furber & Son, to mount with silver fittings one of the feet of the deer from which the haunch was taken. What the Baron thought of this rather unusual gift is not recorded, although he did not retain it for long. On 27 February 1900, when he was made Cheltenham's second Honorary Freeman, he handed it to the Mayor as a gift to the town, having had it set on an ebony base with two match-strikers and an inscribed silver band pierced with holes to hold wax matches. The silver fittings incorporated two inscriptions recording its presentation to the Baron and his subsequent gift of it to the Mayor, along with the coats of arms of Macdonald and de Ferrieres.

After being kept in the Municipal Offices for many years, it was eventually transferred to the Museum.

BARON CHARLES CONRAD Adolphus du Bois de Ferrieres (1823-1908), by John Hanson Walker, 1899. This oval portrait was incorporated in an elaborate wooden frame over one of the doors of the new Art Gallery. The Baron was the son of a Belgian industrialist who had settled in England. He served as Cheltenham's Mayor in 1877-1878 and as its MP in 1880-1885.

*The interior of the new Art Gallery, 1899.*

FOR MORE THAN a century, one of the town's leading tobacconists was that established by Frederick Wright (1848-1911), who took over the premises of another tobacconist, F. Hollingsworth, at 112 (now 165) High Street, opposite the Plough Hotel, in 1873. Wrights eventually opened three more branches elsewhere in Cheltenham and at least twelve other shops in towns as far apart as Coventry and Torquay. In 1969, the company was taken over by another chain of tobacconists, and in 1987 the High Street shop was closed.

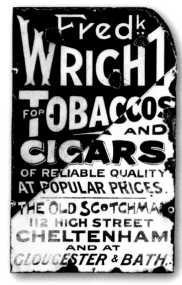

*An enamelled sign advertising Frederick Wright, tobacconist, High Street.*

This late nineteenth-century enamelled sign refers to 'the Old Scotchman', which was the popular name for the wooden figure of a kilted Gordon Highlander taking a pinch of snuff that was put on the pavement outside the shop each morning until the 1960s. The exact age of the figure is uncertain, and it may well have been at the High Street shop when Wright took it over.

In 1987, the new owners removed the Highlander to their head office in London, and in 1990 it was put up for auction and purchased by the family of the late John T. Simmons (died 1966), Frederick Wright's grandson, and a former Managing Director of the company. Since 1991 the figure has been on loan to the Museum, for which parts of the shopfront – including the three glass advertisements and their wooden surrounds that may be seen in the photograph opposite – had been salvaged when the shop was altered in 1987. In 2004, the Museum acquired a second enamelled sign, which was dug up in a Winchcombe garden, plus a large collection of photographs and printed ephemera relating to the company.

*Frederick Wright's trade stand at an exhibition in the Winter Garden, about 1900. An enamelled sign, identical to the Museum's, may be seen on the wall, partly obscured by the table.*

*Number 165 High Street, showing the Highlander, photographed by W.R. Bawden in 1969. (Reproduced by courtesy of the Simmons family)*

89

*The Dowdeswell Pike.*

IN 1878, THE Borough Council purchased the town's private Water Company, which had a reservoir near The Hewletts. Between 1883 and 1886, a much larger reservoir was created at Dowdeswell, to the east of Cheltenham, into which were let the waters of a former fish pond.

On 11 May 1896, the decomposing body of an enormous, apparently blind, female pike, around 4 feet 6 inches long, was found floating on the surface of the reservoir. It was taken to the taxidermist, J.C. White, who mounted and cased the specimen after filling its skin with plaster of Paris. Three years later it became part of the town's embryonic Museum collection.

Research by the Freshwater Biological Association in 1968 concluded that the pike was around thirteen years old at the time of its death and that although its growth rate was normal for the first three years of its life, it grew much faster thereafter. This would seem to confirm that it had been introduced to the reservoir either during or shortly after its construction and that it found an unlimited supply of food in the trout with which the reservoir was stocked for fishing by members of the Council – until blindness meant that that it could no longer catch its prey.

Although the pike may have come from the former fish pond, it has also been suggested that it may have been put into the reservoir by a disgruntled ratepayer, who objected to the Councillors' monopoly of fishing the reservoir!

*The turning of the first sod of the Dowdeswell Reservoir by Mayor George Parsonage, 17 October 1883.*

BECAUSE OF THE plentiful supply of clay underlying Cheltenham, the manufacture of bricks, tiles and pottery was an important industry during the nineteenth century, particularly in Charlton Kings and Leckhampton.

Frederick Thackwell established the Cheltenham Potteries to the south of Naunton Lane (close to the site of the future Leckhampton railway station) in the 1840s, and it was run by his family until 1894, when it was acquired by a Hereford tile manufacturer, Arthur Godwin. In 1897, Godwin moved his entire operation to a new four-acre site in Charlton Lane, which was dominated by a large bottle kiln that could hold up to 20,000 pots.

*An earthenware crock from the Cotswold Potteries, Leckhampton.*

In 1905, the pottery was taken over by new owners, Cotswold Potteries Limited, and it may have been during their period of operation, which ended with the pottery's closure in 1912, that this sixteen-inch high 'red ware' crock was produced. The site of the potteries is now largely occupied by the Leonard Cheshire Home and Charlton Lane Hospital.

The

# Cotswold Potteries
Ltd.

## Leckhampton, Cheltenham.

MANUFACTURERS OF
**Flower Pots, Orchid Pots, Garden Vases.**
Every description of
Horticultural Ware, Fancy Table Fern Pots.
**Washing and Bread Pans.**
Artistic Green and Red Glazed Goods.
**Guinea & Half-Guinea Hampers for Bazaars, &c.**
The largest or smallest quantities of our goods are supplied, and we respectfully solicit enquiries and inspection of the works.

*An advertisement for the Cotswold Potteries Ltd, from* The Way About Cheltenham, *1908.*

THE GLOUCESTERSHIRE DAIRY was
established by Mary Butler (later Mrs
Holborow) at 7 Clarence Street in 1879,
and moved to 2 (now 23) Promenade,
opposite Cavendish House, in 1881. As
well as being the firm's shop, offices and
bottling centre, the new premises had
a popular roof-garden café. By 1894 the
dairy had opened a branch at 15 Suffolk
Parade, and eventually had a large model
dairy in Imperial Lane and at least eight
other shops in Cheltenham and beyond,
as well as several dairy farms at Charlton
Kings and Prestbury.

*A Gloucestershire Dairy
Company stoneware cream pot.*

The dairy became a limited company
in 1914, and had changed its name to the
Gloucestershire Dairy Company & Creamery Ltd by 1933. It later
acquired the Cheltenham Creamery (1939) and Cheltine Foods
(about 1941) and added baking to its dairy business. Baking ceased in
1971 and the milk business was sold to Express Dairies in 1993, but
the name 'Cheltine Ltd' was retained as that of an investment and
property management company.

This four-inch high stoneware cream pot, which was dug up in a
Cheltenham garden, probably dates from before 1914 and is one of a
number of items relating to local dairies in the Museum's collection.
The others include milk bottles and one of the colourful pony traps
that were once a familiar sight in the town as their drivers went about
delivering milk. The trap, once used by W. Griffiths of Pittville Circus
Road, was returned to Cheltenham from a Herefordshire barn in 2003.

*An advertisement for
the Gloucestershire
Dairy Company, from
Cheltenham Illustrated:
The Garden Town of
England, 1889.*

*A Borough of Cheltenham South African War Certificate, 1901.*

CHELTENHAM'S TWO WAR memorials in the Promenade Long Garden – one to the second Boer War of 1899-1902, and the other to the two world wars and beyond – recall the many Cheltenham people who served, or died, during successive conflicts.

In July 1901, the Borough Council resolved to 'place on record its appreciation of the gallant and patriotic services rendered by Townsmen who have served in South Africa, its congratulation and welcome to those who have had the happiness to return to their homes, and its sincere condolence with the relatives and friends of those who have lost their lives in the service of their country…and that a Copy of it under Seal, and suitably inscribed, be presented to each returned Member of the Forces and to the parents or other near relatives of those who have died abroad during the War'.

The certificate was designed by the local artist and publisher Edward Burrow, and shows 'Cheltonia' welcoming a soldier home. The Museum has three examples of the certificate; the one shown above was awarded to Private Samuel Hooper, a Reservist with the 1st Gloucestershire Regiment, who was awarded the Queen's South Africa Medal with clasps for the Orange Free State, Transvaal and Natal. The certificates were clearly not all awarded at the same time as they are each signed by one of two successive Mayors, George Norman (served 1898-1901) and Richard Rogers (served 1901-1903).

The South African War Memorial, of which a postcard is shown on the right, was unveiled in July 1907; puzzlingly, Samuel Hooper's name is not included, although that of one E. Hooper is.

*A programme and two medals for Cheltenham's 1902 Coronation celebrations.*

THE MUSEUM HAS a good collection of printed ephemera and ceramics relating to the local celebration of Royal events from the accession of Queen Victoria in 1837 to the Diamond Jubilee of 2012.

One such event was the Coronation of King Edward VII and Queen Alexandra in 1902, which was originally scheduled for 26 June, but which had to be postponed until 9 August, after the King came down with appendicitis two days before the ceremony.

This programme for the town's 1902 Coronation celebrations details all the day's events, from the ringing of St Mary's Church bells at 8 a.m. to an afternoon Horse Parade and an evening Fancy Dress Cycle Parade. Bands played at various locations throughout the day, and entertainments and sports competitions were held in Montpellier Gardens, Pittville Park and Naunton Park.

Around 2,000 of the town's 'aged poor', nominated by the local clergy, each received a two-shilling voucher to spend on food or clothing in the town's shops, and 9,000 bronze commemorative medals were produced by Martin & Co., and distributed to pupils at the town's elementary schools. Unfortunately, the medals, two examples of which are shown above, were struck before the King's illness and therefore have the wrong date for the Coronation!

THE CHELTENHAM LADIES' College was founded in 1853, and held its first classes in February 1854, at Cambray House, the site of which is now occupied by Cambray Court flats. In 1873, the College moved to a new building at the corner of Montpellier Street and St George's Road, and further buildings were added along Montpellier Street between 1876 and 1898.

*A Cheltenham Ladies' College Jubilee medallion, 1904.*

In 1904, to mark the fiftieth anniversary of its opening, the sculptor and medallist Lilian Vereker Hamilton (whose sister, Daisy Swainson, taught art at the College) produced an oval medallion with a profile portrait of Dorothea Beale (1831-1906), who had served as the College's Principal since 1858, and who continued to do so until her death. Miss Beale is shown in her academic cap, while the reverse bears the dates 1854-1904 and is inscribed 'In Commemoration of the Jubilee of the Cheltenham Ladies College Cheltenham', with the College motto *Coelesti Luce Crescat* ('May She Grow in Heavenly Light'). Silver and bronze versions were produced, and sold for 7s 6d and 5s 6d respectively, 25 per cent of the proceeds being donated to the College.

In November 1904, the College Guild presented to the College a portrait of Miss Beale by James Shannon RA, and in May 1905 a group of well-wishers from outside the College presented a marble bust of Miss Beale by the local sculptor J.E. Hyett, which was funded by public subscription. Both may still be seen in the College.

Although 1904 marked the actual anniversary, the main celebrations, including a Jubilee Service and Concert, were delayed until 12-13 May 1905, in order to coincide with the opening of the College's new Science Wing, facing St George's Road.

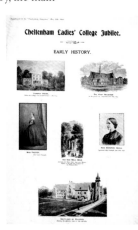

*The front page of a photographic supplement to the* Cheltenham Examiner, *issued on 17 May 1905 to mark the Ladies' College Jubilee celebrations. It shows views of Cambray House, the two earliest Montpellier Street buildings, the Well Walk and the College's first two Principals, Miss Procter and Miss Beale.*

*An advertisement for a recital by the violinist Marie Hall, 1905.*

ONE OF THE many renowned musicians who have lived in Cheltenham is the violinist Marie Hall (1884-1956), to whom the composer Ralph Vaughan Williams dedicated one of his best-known works, *The Lark Ascending* (1914), which she premiered in 1920.

Marie Hall's first public performance was in 1902, and she first appeared in Cheltenham the following year. She settled in the town in 1911 after marrying her Manager, Edward Baring, whose theatrical and event management business, Baring Brothers, was based there. The couple lived at 9 Eldorado Road for the rest of their lives, and a blue plaque now records her time there.

Marie and Edward had one daughter, Pauline Baring (1911-1971), who became an accomplished pianist and often performed with her mother. After her mother's death, she moved to 107 Charlton Lane, where, following her death, the new occupants of the house found three boxes containing a large archive relating not only to Marie Hall, but to many other performances and events in Cheltenham and beyond between 1903 and 1947. These were then given to the Museum, and comprise posters, programmes, tickets, photographs and scrapbooks, among them this advertisement for a recital at the Winter Garden (here spelt 'Gardens') in 1905.

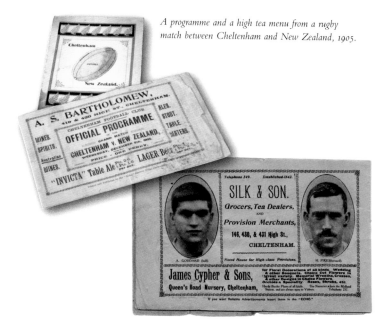

*A programme and a high tea menu from a rugby match between Cheltenham and New Zealand, 1905.*

BETWEEN SEPTEMBER 1905 and February 1906, the New Zealand Rugby Team undertook a tour of Britain, Ireland, France and North America, winning all but one of their thirty-six matches, the only team to beat them being the Welsh Rugby Team. It was during this tour that the name 'All Blacks' was first applied to them, although whether this was from the colour of their kit, or from a newspaper misprint, describing them as 'all blacks' rather than 'all backs' is still debated!

Thirty-two of their matches were played in Britain and Ireland, including, on 6 December 1905, a match against Cheltenham Rugby Football Club at the Athletic Ground in Albion Street, the site of which is now occupied by Tom Price Close. A capacity crowd of over 7,000 saw Cheltenham beaten 18-0.

One of the forwards in the Cheltenham team was a thirty-year-old printer named Harry Pike. In 1974, his son, Mr A.H. Pike, gave the Museum a number of items relating to the match that the family had kept since 1905. They include a copy of the official programme and the menu for a high tea held at the Town Hall after the match. A page from the programme, including a photograph of Harry Pike, is shown above.

*A pair of ice skates used on Pittville Lake.*

PITTVILLE PARK HAS been one of the town's major recreational areas since its creation by the Borough Council between 1888 and 1892. That process began in 1888 with the purchase of land for a Recreation Ground (later named after James Agg-Gardner, who gave the Council the £3,000 needed to acquire it) and continued with the purchase of Pittville Gardens in 1890 and the Marle Hill Lake in 1892.

The two lakes in particular formed an important facility in the Park – for boating in summer and for ice skating during those winters in which the lakes froze over.

This pair of ice skates is believed to have been used at Pittville, and are almost identical to a pair being worn by the boy seated on a bench by the upper lake (created as part of Joseph Pitt's Pittville Estate in the late 1820s) in the photograph above, which is taken from a magic lantern slide.

MAUD'S ELM WAS a large tree in Swindon Road, which eventually reached a height of 80 feet and a girth of 21 feet, and around which one of Cheltenham's most enduring legends developed, namely that of the unfortunate Maud Bowen.

According to the story, which seems to have first appeared in the *Cheltenham Looker-On* for August 1836, Maud Bowen was a young woman from Swindon Village who was found drowned nearby, close to the body of her uncle, who had an arrow through his heart. Deemed a murder and suicide, with Maud the likely culprit, she was buried at a crossroads with an elm stake through her body, from which the great tree grew.

*Two candlesticks made from a piece of Maud's Elm.*

Sadly, the true origin of the name is probably far less prosaic, for a number of early maps and documents record it as Mowle's, Maule's or Maul's Elm, perhaps recalling the family of one James Maule, who is recorded in Harper's 1844 Directory as living nearby. Also listed in 1844 are Maule's Cottages, close to the junction of Swindon Lane and St Paul's Road.

Equally sadly, the tree became unsafe after having been struck by lightning in 1906, and it was cut down to a stump in August 1907. All that is now left to recall it are some houses called Maud's Elm, close to its former site, and two items in the Museum's collection – a large block of wood with 'part of Maud's Elm' carved into it and this pair of wooden candlesticks, six inches high, which were given to the Museum in 1942 and which are recorded as having been made 'by Pearce of Fairview' from a piece of the tree.

*Maud's Elm, from a late nineteenth-century magic lantern slide. This view is looking south along Swindon Road toward the town; the houses on the left are now 323-325 Swindon Road.*

BETWEEN 6 AND 11 JULY 1908, Cheltenham staged the Gloucestershire Historical Pageant, a series of eight re-enactments of English history from the Roman invasion to the visit of King George III to Cheltenham in 1788. The Pageant, which involved 3,000 performers, was held in the grounds of Marle Hill House, overlooking the lower lake at Pittville, opposite which a grandstand for 4,000 spectators was erected.

*A bone china dish from the 1908 Gloucestershire Historical Pageant.*

The Museum has a number of souvenirs of the Pageant, including photographs, postcards, souvenir programmes and one item from what was probably a set of crested china that was produced for the Pageant organisers by Carlton China of Stoke-on-Trent. It is a small dish, three inches across, with the Pageant crest in the centre. As well as the manufacturer's stamp, this example is stamped with the mark of W.H. Rhodes, who is recorded as a china dealer at 5 Promenade Villas between 1908 and 1911.

A Souvenir of the Gloucestershire Historical Pageant, Cheltenham, July 6th to 11th, 1908.

One Shilling.

EDWARD J. BURROW, Royal Publishing Office, Cheltenham.

*The cover of a Souvenir of the Gloucestershire Historical Pageant.*

*A group of Cheltenham Racecourse Steeplechase Club badges, 1910-1935.*

HORSE RACING HAS played an important part in Cheltenham's
sporting and social life at various times since the town's first race
meeting was held on Nottingham Hill, north of the town, in 1815. In
1831, after some years at Cleeve Hill, the races moved for the first time
to Prestbury Park, and they returned there again in 1847-1853, and
have been held there continuously since 1898.

Many of the familiar elements of the present racing programme were
introduced during the early twentieth century, including the National
Hunt Festival, held at Cheltenham in 1902-1905 and again continuously
since 1911, and the Gold Cup and Champion Hurdle, which were first
held at Cheltenham in 1924 and 1927 respectively.

In 1907, the exclusive Steeplechase Club was established, for
whose members a club lounge was provided in the new grandstand
that was opened in 1908. These metal members' badges – of which
the Museum has twenty-eight examples dating from between 1910
and 1936 – were produced each year. Although gentlemen could
become full members for a two guinea 'entrance fee' and an annual
subscription of five guineas, ladies could only be honorary members,
at a reduced rate, and even they were limited to widows or to what
the rules described as 'independent single ladies not living with
parents'. In both cases, members could bring one other lady visitor
with them. In 1911, of the 336 members, only twenty-two were ladies.

*A trade label for Barnett White,*
*taxidermist, Upper Bath Road.*

FROM THE MID-NINETEENTH century onwards, a succession of
taxidermists named White worked in Cheltenham, beginning with
Thomas White (1818-1876) of 86 Upper Bath Road (also known as
10 Norwood Terrace). After his death, his widow Mary, and his second
son, George Job White (born 1845) continued the business until it was
sold in 1900. The Museum has a cased albino mole for which Thomas
White & Son were awarded first prize and medal by the Gloucester
and Cheltenham Ornithological Society in 1865.

Another of Thomas's sons, Barnett (1850-1945) also took up
taxidermy, although he is recorded in census returns until 1901 as a
carpenter and builder. He is listed in directories as a taxidermist and
naturalist at 86 Upper Bath Road from 1905 onwards, which helps to
date this trade label.

In 1883, the eleven-year-old Edward Wilson was given his first
lessons in taxidermy by 'White the bird stuffer', an instruction
that certainly stood him in good stead during his two Antarctic
expeditions. Unfortunately it is not known which of the Whites this
refers to. It is probably too early to be Barnett, and although it may
be George, it could also be one Henry White (born 1823), who is
recorded as a 'bird preserver' at 2 St Luke's Terrace from 1871 onwards,
or even his son, James Charles White (1863-1930), who is also
recorded as such in 1881, and who later served as Assistant Curator at
the Cheltenham College Museum.

This trade label is pasted on the reverse of a wooden shield, nine
inches by six inches, which one assumes once held a mounted
specimen, although that has long since disappeared.

*A plaster maquette for the statue of Shakespeare on the pediment of Cheltenham Library, 1911.*

Right *The Library and Museum, showing the statue of Shakespeare, 1927.*

CHELTENHAM'S FREE LIBRARY and Schools of Art & Science were opened at the corner of St George's Place and Clarence Street on 24 April 1889. At the centre of the building, high above its main entrance, was a parapet on which an eight-foot high Bath stone statue of Shakespeare was placed in May 1911.

The statue shows the poet in a plain tunic and hose, with a long cloak. In one hand he holds a manuscript, and in the other a quill pen. The statue was the gift of Mr R. W. Boulton, the son of the leading Cheltenham sculptor, Richard Lockwood Boulton, one of whose employees, Alfred George Hailing (1879-1947), was responsible for modelling it.

This plaster maquette for the model, which is three feet high, was given to the Museum from the estate of Mr Hailing's daughter in 2003.

DURING THE FIRST World War, eight major Red Cross or Voluntary Aid Detachment hospitals were opened in Cheltenham, at which wounded soldiers were cared for. The hospitals were sited in a number of exist-ing buildings, namely at the Racecourse, three schools, two College boarding houses and a number of private homes, including New Court in Lansdown Road, whose owner, Mr J. Fleming, offered it to the War Office soon after the outbreak of war.

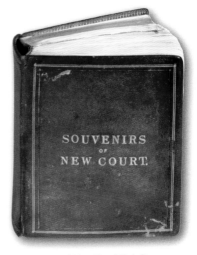

*'Souvenirs of New Court' Red Cross Hospital, 1915-1917.*

In all, 15,852 soldiers were nursed in the town's VAD hospitals between 1914 and 1919, 1,697 of them at New Court, which operated between 21 October 1914 and 18 December 1918. Among the volunteers at New Court during the years 1915-1917 was Miss Dorothy Unwin, whose father, Herbert Unwin of Arle Court, was a great supporter of the hospitals and who paid for a new wooden ward to be built at New Court in 1916, thereby increasing its number of beds by twenty-two.

During her time at New Court, Miss Unwin compiled this fascinating 'scrapbook', with a mixture of photographs, newspaper cuttings, entertainment programmes, cartoons and signed messages of appreciation from many of the hospital's patients. What happened to the book after 1917 is uncertain, but it was eventually acquired by the Cheltenham antique dealer Ron Summerfield, whose trustees gave it to the Museum after his death in 1989.

The photograph above shows the tooled leather cover of the book, while opposite is a typical page from the book, and a photograph of some of the staff, taken on Easter Monday 1917.

DURING THE FIRST World War, the people of Cheltenham invested around £2,250,000 in War Bonds and Savings Certificates. In recognition of this, the Treasury presented the local War Savings Association with a tank, which arrived at St James's Station on 21 May 1919 in order to make its way to Westal Green, at the junction of Lansdown Road and Queen's Road, for a presentation ceremony at 3.30 p.m.

All, however, did not go according to plan. Once offloaded at the station, the tank refused to start, and when it finally did, it misfired and came to a halt twice, in Bayshill Road and near the Gordon Lamp at Lansdown. By the time it finally reached Westal Green, well over an hour late, the presentation speeches were over! In apologising for its late arrival, the National War Savings Committee's representative, Captain Forster, somewhat ungallantly noted that there were two types of tanks – lady tanks and gentleman tanks – and that, as it was late, this must have been a lady tank!

This poster advertises both the Presentation Event and Tank Week generally, during which people were encouraged to invest further in bonds and certificates, in return for which they would be invited to view the interior of the tank.

The tank remained at Westal Green until 1927, when it was removed to Montpellier Gardens, to make way for the electricity sub-station that still stands at Westal Green today. Thirteen years later it was sent for scrap as part of the next war effort.

*A Cheltenham Tank Week poster, 1919.*

*A cartoon by George Wilson Fenning, from the* Cheltenham Looker-On, *showing the Mayor, Alderman John Bendall, welcoming investors to the tank. The reference to this being the first 'real' tank recalls the fact that a near full-size model of a tank had toured the town during December 1918 as part of the war savings effort. (Reproduced by courtesy of Cheltenham Local & Family History Centre)*

ONE OF CHELTENHAM'S leading industrial concerns during the late nineteenth and early twentieth century was H.H. Martyn & Company, which gained a worldwide reputation for high quality craftsmanship in wood, stone, bronze, iron, plaster and stained glass.

Founded in 1888 by Herbert Henry Martyn (1842-1937), who came to Cheltenham from Worcester

*'The Limber - A Broken Pole', a sculpture by Robert Lindsey Clark, 1924.*

in 1866 to work for the stonemason R.L. Boulton, the company's first premises were at a house called Sunningend, at the corner of High Street and College Road. In 1908, the company moved to far larger premises by Lansdown railway station (including William Letheren's former Vulcan Iron Works), which it also named Sunningend. The company retained its independent existence there until 1934, when it was taken over by Maples, the London furnishers, and it was finally closed in 1971.

The Museum has an extensive collection of material relating to the company and its employees, including one of at least four known bronze castings of what is believed to be an unsuccessful entry in an open competition to design a war memorial for the Promenade in 1919. Entitled 'The Limber – A Broken Pole', it was designed by the company's head sculptor and art director, Robert Lindsey Clark (1864-1926), and shows an eighteen-pounder gun limber of the Royal Horse Artillery, whose rider is attempting to pull the carriage out of the mud after one of its limber poles has broken.

The sculptures were cast in 1924, in which year one of them was exhibited at the Royal Academy, where, according to one report, 'it won universal admiration for its spirited and bold design, its remarkably life-like movement, as well as for the excellent craftsmanship embodied in its execution'. Between 1926 and 1928, the Museum organised a successful appeal to raise £250 in order to purchase 'No. 4 Replica' from the artist's widow, and to commission Martyns to produce a walnut and ebony base, with a bronze plaque, on which it still stands.

*An advertisement card for Alfred Miles Ltd, Carriage and Motor Body Builders, Winchcombe Street.*

THE CARRIAGE AND Motor Body Builders, Alfred Miles Ltd, was founded in 1860 by a Stroud-born coach builder named Samuel Miles, whose son Alfred (1853-1932) was born while his father was working in Salisbury. Exactly when Alfred succeeded his father is uncertain, but he is listed in the 1881 census as a coach builder employing four men and four boys at 19 Albion Street. In 1897, he opened a new showroom in Winchcombe Street, where the company was still operating at the time of his retirement sometime after 1912. By then, like so many coach builders, the company had also become motor engineers, as shown in this 1920s advertising leaflet.

The Museum has one vehicle manufactured by Alfred Miles – a horse-drawn, two-wheeled 'Governess' cart or tub of about 1900.

Following Alfred's retirement, his son Felix (1891-1972) managed the business, which was eventually acquired by the Hawker Siddeley Group in 1959. Alfred Miles himself devoted the latter part of his retirement to the compilation of a monumental ten-volume 'scrapbook' history of Cheltenham, begun in 1925 and given to Cheltenham Library following his death. Now in Gloucestershire Archives, it still forms a valuable resource for local historians.

ONE OF THE most famous actresses ever to appear in Cheltenham was the French actress Sarah Bernhardt (1844-1923), who gave two performances at the Town Hall on 24 April 1916, as part of a short provincial tour following a successful London season. Her performance comprised several recitations, and her own one-act play, entitled *Du Theatre au Champ d'Honneur* ('From the Theatre to the Field of Honour') in which she took the part of a wounded French soldier at the Western Front.

*A silver card case presented to Sarah Bernhardt at the Town Hall, 1916.*

Her performances had been arranged by Samuel C. Field, the lessee of the Winter Garden, and it was perhaps Field who presented her with this card case as a token of gratitude for what the *Cheltenham Looker-On* described as 'the greatest booking of the year'. It was probably all the more so given that Bernhardt was seventy-two years of age and had undergone a leg amputation the previous year, as a result of complications from a fall on stage ten years earlier.

The card case was hallmarked at Chester in 1899, and the makers' mark is that of George Nathan and Ridley Hayes of Birmingham. What happened to it after 1916 is not known, but in 1983 it came up for auction in Cheltenham and was purchased by the Museum.

*Sarah Bernhardt, who was often known as 'the Divine Sarah', photographed by H. Walter Barnett, 1910. (© National Portrait Gallery, London)*

THE PROMENADE'S ROLE as the town's leading shopping street began with the establishment of Thomas Clark and William Debenham's 'Cavendish House Silk Mercery' in 1826 and has continued ever since. The widespread reputation of 'the Prom' was such that a 1926 guidebook to the town could justifiably refer to it as 'the Bond Street of the West'.

*A cardboard box from Walter Ayris, costumier, dressmaker and furrier, Promenade.*

One of the Promenade's leading stores during the first half of the twentieth century was that of Walter Ayris (1867-1935), who opened a ladies' outfitters at 14 Promenade Villas in 1899 and later established tailoring workshops in Ormond Place. In 1939, the firm became a limited company, and in 1951 it was acquired by Cavendish House, into whose premises it later moved.

This cardboard box, which is a little over sixteen inches wide, was sent to a customer in Minchinhampton in 1927, and, as the label reveals, was later used to house a collection of dolls. The box was eventually passed to Stroud's Museum in the Park, which transferred it to Cheltenham in 2011.

*Ayris's fine shopfront in the Promenade, with the Municipal Offices reflected in its windows, by an unknown photographer, about 1940. (Reproduced by courtesy of Jill Julier)*

ALTHOUGH THE HEYDAY of the Cheltenham waters was over by the mid-nineteenth century, they have continued to be available ever since, either at the Town Hall's Central Spa (opened in 1906, but not currently operating), at the Pittville Pump Room, or for a time during the early twentieth century, bottled as the 'Chelspa' Cheltenham Natural Aperient Water.

Chelspa Water was one of a large number of medical and toilet products that were produced by the United Chemists' Association Ltd (UCAL), which was originally established in Sheffield in 1904, but moved to Cheltenham in about 1912.

*Two Chelspa Natural Aperient Water bottles.*

In its heyday after the Second World War, UCAL employed about 300 people at its factory in Corpus Street. The firm later moved to the Kingsditch Industrial Estate, but closed following a company takeover in 1972.

Chelspa Water was stated on the label to be 'guaranteed by over 1000 British pharmacists'. It was recommended for a remarkable range of complaints, including eczema, epilepsy, gout, migraine, obesity and 'for derangements of stomach, bowels, and liver, due to indiscretion in diet and drink'. The label featured the Borough's coat of arms and the 1789 Royal Cheltenham and Restoration Medal, the latter no doubt to establish the water's historic pedigree.

The Museum has a number of other examples of UCAL's products, including hair lotion and bandages, which at the company's height were retailed through a network of more than 6,000 independent pharmacists.

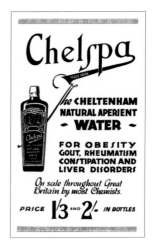

*An advertisement for Chelspa Natural Aperient Water, from* The Charm of Cheltenham Spa, *1935.*

*The Cheltenham Tram.*

CHELTENHAM'S PUBLIC TRANSPORT system has gone from sedan chairs to horse-drawn omnibuses to electric trams, which were operated by the Cheltenham and District Light Railway Company between 1901 and 1930. The first line to be opened was that between Lansdown and Cleeve Hill, in August 1901, with further lines to Leckhampton and Charlton Kings in 1905.

In 1921, the company added three new vehicles to its fleet, purchased from English Electric at Preston. One of these, Tram 21, is the only one to have survived their scrapping following replacement by motor buses in 1929-1930. After being stored for some years at the company's St Mark's Depot it was purchased for use as a store at Huntscot Farm, Swindon Village, from where its decaying frame was 'rescued' by a group of enthusiasts in 1961.

Between 1961 and 1965, supporters of the Cheltenham 21 Tram Group – including, in 1961, the nineteen-year-old Brian Jones, who was later a founder member of the Rolling Stones – restored the tram to its original condition, and in July 1965 it was transferred to the Tramway Museum Society's collection at Crich in Derbyshire.

A prominent member of the 21 Tram Group was the Assistant Curator of Cheltenham Museum, Graham Teasdill. In 1966, he became the Curator of the Russell-Cotes Museum at Bournemouth, and began to develop a Transport Museum. In 1981, Tram 21 was transferred to Bournemouth, where it was hoped to run it as a working exhibit. That hope was not, however, realised, and in 1992 Bournemouth Borough Council funded its return to Cheltenham, where it arrived at the Council's Swindon Road Depot on 12 March 1992, an event shown in the photograph above.

*A Cheltenham Grammar
School cricket cap, 1928-1929.*

AS THE NUMBER of Cheltenham's schools and colleges increased, so too did the number of its businesses specialising in school uniforms and sports equipment. Among them was that of Thomas Plant (1807-1883), who had opened a hat shop at 345 High Street by 1831. Although the business eventually became a general outfitters, hats, and particularly school caps, remained its most important stock-in-trade. In 1890, *Where to Buy at Cheltenham* noted of Plant's that 'the sale of college caps annually exceeds the output of all other establishments of the town combined'.

In 1892, the shop moved to 18 Colonnade, and it was there that this velvet and silver braid cricket cap was provided for the Grammar School for its 1928/9 year; inside the cap is a label with the shop's name and address. The cap was purchased by the Museum at an auction in 2007, but unfortunately there is no indication of who had originally worn it.

Plant's opened a branch shop in Suffolk Road in 1953, to which its entire business was moved in 1962. In 1988 the shop moved to 198 Bath Road and eventually closed in 1999.

*Part of the interior of Thomas
Plant's Colonnade shop,
from* The Garden Town of
England, *1901.*

BETWEEN 1934 AND 1984, Cheltenham was the 'hub' of the national coach network, a role that had its origins in 'Black & White Luxury Coaches', a small company established in 1926 by George Readings (1893-1981), who had previously run a similar business in Surrey.

Initially operating with a single Reo Sprinter coach (from whose badge the 'winged shield' seen on the company's livery derived), it offered local excursions and a regular service to London, and

*An enamelled Black & White Motorways Ltd. Booking Office sign.*

had a booking office in the High Street (later moved to Paris House in the Promenade) and a garage at Charlton Kings. In 1928, its name was changed to 'Black & White Motorways', and in 1930 – the year in which he sold the business to the Birmingham & Midland Omnibus Company Ltd – George Readings purchased St Margaret's Villa and its three and a half acre garden as the site of a new coach station, which opened in 1931.

In 1934, 'Black & White' (which had retained its separate identity after 1930) became part of an amalgamation of coach companies known as Associated Motorways and the St Margaret's Road coach station was chosen as the hub of the new company's network. So it remained for the next fifty years, even after Associated Motorways had been subsumed into a new national coach company in 1974, at which time 'Black & White' was renamed National Travel (South West). As late as 1983, no less than 598 destinations could be reached from Cheltenham, a figure that shrank to a mere fifty following the end of Cheltenham's interchange role in 1984. The coach station itself eventually closed in 1990, and its buildings were demolished. Its site now serves as a surface car park, pending future redevelopment.

This enamelled sign from the coach station booking office post-dates 1929, the year in which the company took delivery of nine Leyland Tiger TS2 coaches, one of which is shown on the sign. It was given to the Museum by the trustees of the antique dealer, Ron Summerfield, in 1989.

*A wrought iron canopy from the Ellenborough Hotel, Oriel Road, 1929-1930.*

Below *A brochure for the Ellenborough Hotel, showing the canopy, about 1950.*

IN ABOUT 1920, a house at the corner of Oriel Road and Wellington Street that was said to have been Lord Ellenborough's townhouse was converted for use as a hotel, and in 1929-1930 an elaborate wrought iron canopy was installed as part of a portico in front of its entrance. The canopy remained in place until 1972, when the building was demolished to make way for a new office building, Ellenborough House.

At the centre of the canopy was a panel of glass with a coat of arms that was thought (erroneously) to have been that of Lord Ellenborough's family, which had been given to the Museum in 1980. In 2003, the Museum was also able to purchase the canopy itself, which had spent some time in a Birmingham reclamation yard before it was recognised and purchased by a Cheltenham resident. He later sold it to a Cheltenham antique dealer, who offered it to the Museum, which purchased it with financial assistance from the Government Purchase Fund administered by the Victoria & Albert Museum, the Friends of the Art Gallery & Museum and Messrs Rickerbys (Solicitors), who occupied Ellenborough House.

The canopy is the work of Charles William Hancock (1868-1937), one of the town's leading art metalworkers. He trained at William Letheren's Vulcan Iron Works and then became Head of the Wrought Iron Department at Martyns between 1908 and 1925, before setting up his own business in Bennington Street. The Museum also has two other fine examples of his work – a mirror and a framed ornamental panel.

THIS JOINT GREAT Western Railway/London Midland & Scottish Railway poster, showing the Municipal Offices in the Promenade, was published in about 1936. It was designed by Claude Buckle (1905-1973), who is known to have provided the artwork for at least eighty-five posters and twenty-five carriage prints for various railway companies between 1932 and 1963. In this poster he has 'foreshortened' the perspective in order to include the statue of Edward Wilson and part of the Neptune Fountain, both of which are, in fact, opposite the southern end of the terrace

This is one of three known railway posters showing Cheltenham: the other two both show the town from Leckhampton Hill and are by C.H. Birtwhistle (also for the GWR/LMS, 1935) and Douglas Relf (for British Rail, 1945). The Museum also has a copy of the Birtwhistle poster.

*A railway poster showing the Promenade.*
*(© Reproduced by courtesy of Claude Buckle Art)*

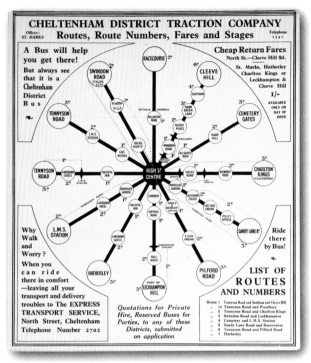

*A Cheltenham District Traction Company bus route plan.*

FROM DECEMBER 1929 onwards, Cheltenham's trams were gradually replaced by a fleet of twenty motor buses, ten of which were open-top double-deckers. Initially their routes more or less coincided with those of the previous electric trams, and this early route plan appears to reflect the routes that were in operation up to February 1932.

Many of the stops and destinations that are shown will still be familiar to bus users today, although the plan refers to several features that have now vanished, including Dicks's in the High Street, Maud's Elm, Calcutta Inn and Lansdown Castle. The latter, the name of which is still applied to a bus stop close to the junction of Lansdown Road and Gloucester Road, recalls the unusual castellated mid-Victorian shop that stood there until its demolition for a road-widening scheme in about 1972. In 1892 it inspired the young Gustav Holst, who gave its name to one of his earliest compositions, an operetta that was first performed at the Cheltenham Corn Exchange in 1893.

DURING THE FIRST World War, H.H.
Martyn & Company produced aircraft
components for a number of aircraft
manufacturers. In 1917, in order to
begin aircraft production in its own
right, it established the Gloucestershire
Aircraft Company, with H.H. Martyn's
son, Alfred W. Martyn, as its first
Chairman. The new company initially
shared Martyns' Sunningend Works,
but it also used an aerodrome on the
Brockworth-Hucclecote boundary,
near Gloucester, to which aircraft

*A model of the Gloster-Whittle E28/39,*
*Britain's first jet-propelled aircraft.*

production was gradually moved from 1925 onwards. In 1926, the
company was renamed the Gloster Aircraft Company (GAC), and it
survived as an independent company until 1961, when it merged with
Armstrong Whitworth.

From 1921 onwards, GAC produced a succession of fighter aircraft,
and two experimental prototypes of the Gloster-Whittle E28/39,
which was to incorporate Frank Whittle's pioneering turbojet engine.
Both were partly assembled in Cheltenham, production having been
moved there due to the threat of bombing at the airfield – the first,
in 1940-1941, at Regent Motors in Regent Street and the second, in
1943, at the former Crabtree Garage in Carlton Street.

This 1:24 scale model of the E28/39 is one of at least four
identical models of the aircraft that have been traced; they may have
been made for presentation to some of those who worked on the
aircraft, perhaps in 1951, when a dinner was held to mark the tenth
anniversary of its first successful flight. Similar models of a number
of other GAC planes are known, examples of four of which are also
included in the Museum's collection.

*The first prototype of the Gloster-*
*Whittle E28/39 on display in the*
*Promenade in April 1946, before its*
*transfer to London's Science Museum.*
*(© Jet Age Museum/Russell Adams*
*Collection)*

*The casing of an unexploded Second World War bomb, 1942.*

DURING THE SECOND World War, Cheltenham suffered a number of air raids, the most significant of which were on the night of 11/12 December 1940, and the early morning of 27 July 1942. In all a total of thirty-four people were killed, and several hundred homes were either damaged or destroyed.

One of the bombs dropped on 27 July 1942, a 500kg SC bomb, landed at the rear of the Ritz Cinema in the Lower High Street (now a bingo hall) but failed to explode. It was defused by the Bomb Disposal Squad of the Dowty Home Guard, and its fuse, tail fin and casing were then put on display in the cinema to raise money for the Military Comforts Fund. The fuse was retained by the officer in charge of the operation, but the empty casing was removed to Dowty's headquarters at Arle Court, where George Dowty later presented each member of the Squad with a small replica of the bomb, inscribed with the recipient's initials and the date of the incident.

The casing remained at Arle Court until the early 1980s, when it was transferred to the Cotswold Aircraft Restoration Group's premises at RAF Innsworth. In 1995, the Group donated the casing to the Museum, following which it was sandblasted and painted in as near as possible its original 'field grey' colour and then installed in the Museum foyer as a donations box; the photograph shows its arrival in the Museum on 20 February 1996. It remained there for several years, until it was transferred, on loan, to the Lower High Street Resource Centre, where it is now used to collect donations towards the Centre's work.

DURING THE SECOND World War, large numbers of American troops were stationed in Cheltenham, which was the headquarters of the American Services of Supply, which occupied many of the town's larger buildings, including the Pittville Pump Room.

On 28 January 1943, as part of a week of fund-raising events for the RAF Benevolent Fund, the 1st Special Service Unit staged an evening's entertainment in the Town Hall, featuring the songs and dances of America's past, from its colonial period to 'swing time' in the 1920s and '30s, culminating in a rendition of both 'God Bless America' and the National Anthem. The cast comprised a chorus of 100 soldiers and a thirty-piece Military Band.

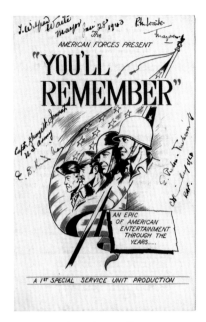

*A programme for an American Forces concert at the Town Hall, 1943.*

According to the *Gloucestershire Echo*, the show 'went with a swing and a zest that swept the audience along from one enjoyment to another', noting in particular when commenting on the section of 'the Gay 90s' that 'the sight of six stalwart soldiers disguised as musical comedy lovelies brought peal after peal of laughter from the audience'.

This programme is signed by a number of those present, including the Unit's Commanding Officer and Cheltenham's Mayor and Mayoress.

THIS SWEET TIN recalls one of twentieth-century Cheltenham's best known manufacturing confectioners, Andy's Candys. The earliest reference to the firm is in 1922, when it was trading at 23 Regent Street, but the sweets themselves are believed to have been made at the Cheltine Foods' Bakery in Chester Walk, behind the Library, Art Gallery & Museum. In 1940, the firm moved to a purpose-built factory in Tewkesbury Road, with adjoining offices in the 'Cotswold vernacular' style. Its grounds, which included a market garden, stretched as far east as Brook Road. It remained there

*An Andy's Candys sweet tin.*

until its closure in 1958, after which its buildings were occupied by Delapena Honing Equipment Ltd, until their demolition in 1997. Its site, at the corner of Tewkesbury Road and Princess Elizabeth Way, is now largely occupied by a motor showroom.

This tin, which is one of two in the Museum's collection, has a rather fanciful 'Memory Picture of the Original Andy's Candy shop', and what became the firm's trademark – a lady in a crinoline dress and bonnet, holding what is presumably a wrapped sweet tin. A concrete version of this figure, about 22 inches high, stood in a niche on the outside wall of the factory, while a smaller plaster version is said to have been sited in the factory's reception area. Both figures survived the firm's closure, and are now in private collections.

*Andy's Candys's offices in Tewkesbury Road, about 1940. (Reproduced by courtesy of Alderman Gil Wakeley)*

IN ADDITION TO its collection of programmes and tickets relating to the various Coronation celebrations that have been held in Cheltenham, the Museum has a number of items relating to Royal visits to the town, including that of Princess Elizabeth – the present Queen Elizabeth II – on 16 March 1951.

The visit had originally been planned for 7 March, to coincide with the National Hunt Festival, which the Princess, along with Queen Elizabeth and Princess Margaret, had planned to attend the following day, but it had to be postponed at short notice, after Princess Elizabeth had come down with a feverish cold: hence the change of date on the Programme.

*A souvenir programme for Princess Elizabeth's visit to Cheltenham, 1951.*

Much of the Princess's visit was taken up with a private visit to Cheltenham College, but later in the day she was driven to the site of the proposed new Hesters Way Estate to 'cut the first turf' and to plant a commemorative tree at what the local press described as 'the town's greatest housing scheme'; the name of the Estate's main Avenue, Princess Elizabeth Way, still recalls the occasion. The Princess also visited one of the town's 'prefabs' on the Alma Road Estate and attended a Reception at the Town Hall.

## CHELTENHAM GRAMMAR SCHOOL

has occupied four build-ings, on two separate sites, since it was founded in 1572. The original sixteenth-century school in the High Street was replaced in 1887-1889 by a new building in the 'Tudor Gothic' style, which was itself replaced by a third school, on a

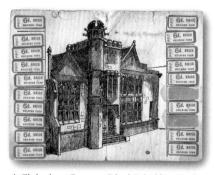

*A Cheltenham Grammar School Rebuilding Fund card, 1961-1962.*

new site in Princess Elizabeth Way, in 1963-1965. That survived until 1996, when it was replaced by the present Pate's Grammar School.

This card was issued by the School's Parents' Association to help raise £25,000 towards the total cost of at least £300,000 that was necessary to build the third school; for every 6d raised, a small sticker to that effect was affixed to the card. This particular card was issued to M.J.E. Peacock, who was a sixth form student in 1961-1962. Perhaps surprisingly, it shows the Victorian school that was to be demolished rather than the new school that was to replace it, possibly because the final designs by the London architects, Chamberlin, Powell & Bon, were not available in time.

The drawing of the Victorian school was the work of John R. Stephens, who was a pupil at the school between 1957 and 1964, and whose drawings were featured in a number of issues of the school magazine, *The Patesian*, from 1961 onwards. In a niche on the front of the building is a statue of the school's founder, Richard Pate, that

was removed before the building was demolished and later incorporated into both the 1965 and 1996 buildings.

*The 1963-5 Grammar School, by an unknown photographer. (Reproduced by courtesy of Pate's Grammar School)*

*A 'Chelt Ales' beer bottle and tray.*

THE CHELTENHAM ORIGINAL Brewery's premises on the north side of the High Street were gradually enlarged during the nineteenth century, but apart from the large, late 1860s malt house that still survives at the corner of Henrietta Street and St Margaret's Road, were almost totally destroyed by fire in 1897, following which they were rebuilt in fireproof materials.

The company underwent a series of name changes during the twentieth century, as it either acquired, or merged with, other breweries. In 1945, it purchased the Hereford & Tredegar Brewery and became Cheltenham & Hereford Breweries Ltd, and in 1956 it merged with the Stroud Brewery Company Ltd to form West Country Brewery Holdings, which itself became part of Whitbread Flowers in 1963. Whitbreads continued to operate the brewery until its closure in 1998, following which much of its site was redeveloped for retail premises, although retaining parts of the nineteenth-century buildings.

Throughout its life the brewery has produced a series of distinctive products, not least its various 'Chelt Ales', which are recalled by this (unopened) beer bottle and tray, both of which date from the 1960s.

THE GROCERS A. Whittern & Son, at the corner of Suffolk Road and Suffolk Parade, was established in 1932 by Allan Whittern, in premises that had been occupied as a grocer's shop since at least 1850.

During the early 1960s, a signwriter from the Whitbread Artists' Department painted the shop's back door with a life-size portrait of Mr Whittern holding a wooden Whitbread's crate; quoted in the *Gloucestershire Echo* in January 1992, Mr Whittern's son

*A painted door from A. Whittern & Son, grocers, Suffolk Parade.*

recalled the signwriter 'asking dad what he wanted on the door and he said "oh, just put a picture of me there" as a joke – and he did!'

The door was a familiar sight to shoppers in that part of the town, as was the shop's traditional interior with its mahogany counters, behind which customers were served by staff in traditional long white aprons.

Parts of the portrait were retouched or repainted in the following years by one or more artists from the Cheltenham-based Brewery Artists, which was established following the closure of the Whitbread Artists' Department; this included the replacement of the wooden crate with a plastic one some time in the 1980s.

Allan Whittern ran the business until his death in 1982, when it was taken over by his son, Allan Whittern, who continued in business until its closure in December 1991, following which the door was removed to the Museum before the shop was re-fitted.

*Mr Allan Whittern outside his shop in 1991. (Photograph by courtesy of Michael Charity Photography)*

*A model of Eagle Star House, Bath Road.*

FOLLOWING THE SECOND World War, a number of major organisations relocated to Cheltenham, including the Eagle Star Insurance Company's administrative head office and computer centre, for which a striking new thirteen-storey hexagonal office building, 161 feet high, was officially opened in October 1968. A further extension was added, at ground level, in 1981.

The building was designed by the London architects, Stone, Toms and Partners, and cost £1.7 million. Its site covered 2.5 acres, the acquisition of which involved the purchase and demolition of several early nineteenth-century houses, although two – Montpellier House and Atherstone Lawn – were retained for the company's use and renamed Eagle Lodge and Star Lodge respectively.

In 1998, Eagle Star became part of Zurich Financial Services, and the Tower was renamed UK Life Tower. In 2003, Zurich sold the building, since when it has been occupied by a number of different companies.

This model of Eagle Star House was made by Archley Models of Watford, presumably for the architects. It was given to the Museum by Zurich Financial Services in 2003 and is one of four models of the town's more recent buildings that are held by the Museum, the others being of the Magistrates' Court in St George's Road, the Swimming Pool at Pittville and the Quadrangle in Imperial Square.

If you enjoyed this book, you may also be interested in …

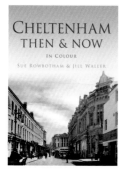

## Cheltenham Then & Now

SUE ROWBOTHAM & JILL WALLER

Featuring 45 scenes of yesteryear with 45 modern colour views, this book reveals what has been lost and what remains. Drawing on detailed local knowledge of the community and illustrated with a wealth of fascinating images, this book recalls what has changed in Cheltenham in terms of buildings, traditions and ways of life.

978 0 7524 6527 2

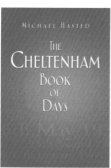

## The Cheltenham Book of Days

MICHAEL HASTED

Featuring all sort of events – humourous, tragic, historical and political – *The Cheltenham Book of Days* is filled with an astonishing range of material. Whether it be the visits of Jane Austen or Lord Byron, the birth of Rolling Stone Brian Jones or the actor Sir Ralph Richardson or the invention of the jet engine, not a day has gone by which is not worthy of attention. Dip into this fascinating collection and celebrate the town's phenomenal history.

978 0 7524 6544 9

## Haunted Cheltenham

DIZ WHITE

This collection of chilling tales from Cheltenham includes eerie stories of a Civil War spook, a spinet-playing shade, a time-stealing sprite and a bedroom-wrecking banshee. Also featured are tales from Prestbury, reputedly the most haunted village in Britain. Illustrated with over sixty atmospheric photographs, this book is a must for everyone interested in Cheltenham and the paranormal.

978 0 7524 5427 6

Visit our website and discover thousands of other History Press books.

**www.thehistorypress.co.uk**